CW01496492

Experiences of Positive Gay Identity

Beyond Coming Out

Experiences of Positive Gay Identity

Kevin Alderson, Ph.D, C. Psych.

Edited by Kate Harding.
Copy edited by Maria Lundin.
Designed by Mike O'Connor.

Canadian Cataloguing in Publication Data

Alderson, Kevin George, 1956-
  Beyond coming out: experiences of positive gay identity

ISBN 1-895837-57-X

1. Gay men. 2. Gays - Identity. I. Title.

HQ76.A42 2000   305.9'06642   C00-930475-4

The publisher gratefully acknowledges the support of the Canada Council, the Ontario Arts Council and Department of Canadian Heritage through the Book Publishing Industry Development Program.

Printed and bound in Canada

Insomniac Press, 192 Spadina Avenue, Suite 403,
Toronto, Ontario, Canada, M5T 2C2
www.insomniacpress.com

To the gay men in my life who taught me what it means to have a positive gay identity.

To Garry Johnson, my late friend and mentor, who epitomized it.

To Kevin, my partner, who still does.

Contents

Author's Note

If we wait until we are not afraid to speak, we will be speaking from our graves. (Lorde, 1984, cited in O'Conor, 1995, p. 15)

This book is about the experience of gay men who have developed positive gay identities. I did not study the experience of lesbians, whose experience I know can be equally tumultuous, or worse. As a man, I felt the experience of women would be better studied by another woman. I hope this book will inspire someone to undertake this challenge. It is important work that needs to be done.

Most of the individuals in this book have suffered, silenced by a secret code in a society that only recently has allowed gay people to give voice to what their hearts have told them for years. Initially plagued by repression and denial, these gay men have broken free, subsequently finding deep meaning in their experience. This is a book that describes their journeys — uncensored.

Do you know what it takes to activate the defense mechanisms of repression and denial? Basically a lot of trauma. Our minds only shut out pieces of reality when that reality is too painful to accept. Although the situation is changing, the traditional values of mainstream society regarding gay people have been extremely negative. More than half of gay men have been verbally harassed or physically assaulted because of their sexual orientation.[1] The barrage of negative attitudes and discriminatory acts against gay individuals have resulted in symptoms of emotional abuse among homosexuals.

It is well documented that when emotional abuse is consistently levied against a child the child grows up with feelings of self-hatred and low self-esteem. You can only throw rocks so long before a child's spirit is shattered. The same holds true for anyone subjected to systematic cruelty.

The rocks thrown at gay people have struck their targets. The cost of homophobia and heterosexist thinking is staggering to our young people — both have been associated with school problems, running away from home, substance abuse, and prostitution.[2] Gay male adolescents have a higher rate of attempted suicide than non-gay youth as well.[3] Although gay youth develop the same as heterosexuals biologically, their emotional and social development is often impaired,[4] which likely results from their inability to date others of the same gender.

Gay adults cannot escape the effects of society's abuse either. Many do not come out until they are well into adulthood, and then suffer something akin to a "delayed adolescence."[5] This is analogous to being a teenager trapped inside an adult body. Emotional development has been delayed as these men have not had the opportunity to develop gay relationships, the only kind of romantic relationships from which they can derive fulfillment.

Other evidence suggests that not accepting one's gayness may be causally related to the high incidence of alcohol abuse and dependence witnessed in the gay community.[6] As you will read later, many individuals interviewed for this book experienced drug and alcohol problems as well. Furthermore, the incidence of public sex (e.g., sex in washrooms) is highest in communities most opposed to homosexuality and among individuals who repress and are in denial.[7] Those who deny and repress are more likely to "act out" their desires in socially unacceptable, if not blatantly criminal, ways.

This book is not about repression and denial. It goes *beyond* that. It takes us to the place where our society should have been all along. That place is a loving land where we accept people for who and what they are. Canada is moving that way, but the stories here are those of gay men whose souls have already soared to that better place.

Kevin Alderson, Ph.D.
Chartered Psychologist
March 1, 2000

Studying Positive Gay Identity

As I slowly reconstructed my sense of self after coming out,[8] I often paused and wondered if everyone had found it this difficult. As I tried to understand what it meant to be gay, I read about and met other gay men. It struck me that although the gay community is quite diverse, there is a qualitative difference between those who have come to rejoice as gay men and those who regret their gay identity to some extent. How, then, do some people "break free" and begin to live happy lives as gay men?

The content for this book evolved from the dissertation I worked on for three years.

I sought an answer to my research question, which became, **"What is the experience of men who construct and integrate a positive gay identity?"** The next section briefly explains how I answered it.

The Power of Stories

But stories! Stories are the vehicle that moves metaphor and image into experience. Like metaphors and images, stories communicate what is generally invisible and ultimately inexpressible. In seeking to understand these realities through time, stories provide a perspective that touches on the divine, allowing us to see reality in full context, as part of its larger whole. Stories invite a kind of vision that gives shape and form even to the invisible, making the images move, clothing the metaphors, throwing color into the shadows. Of all the devices available to us, stories are the surest way of touching the human spirit.
(Kurtz & Ketcham, 1996, p. 17).

As a young child, I watched people's reactions while they rode a roller-coaster. The unnerving screams I heard seemed inconsistent with the look of exhilaration and pleasure on their faces once the ride ended. Was this insanity, or merely the relief one experiences after surviving such a torturous ordeal?

Now, as a psychologist, I know there are different ways to study reactions to a roller-coaster. There are physiological measures, like changes in pulse or body temperature. Psychological measurements might include comparing the traits of individuals who ride roller-coasters with those who don't, or measuring their subjective reactions on rating scales.

Another approach would involve interviewing riders soon after they get off the roller-coaster. Hearing more about their experience, I could begin to really understand what it might be like to take that ride. There is still a distance between me and that phenomenon, however, because I am still trying to understand from the perspective of the other.

If I *really* want to know what it's like to ride a roller-coaster, I have to get on it. Now, the unnerving screams I hear are my own—so is the look of exhilaration and pleasure on my face once the ride ends. I may still interview others who have also ridden roller-coasters, but nothing can replace the tacit knowledge I've gained through this experience. The choice, then, is whether to ignore it or acknowledge it in my investigation. For the purposes of this book, I decided on the latter.

Deciding who to interview was challenging, although I had been considering potential *co-researchers*[9] for two years. Through my social life and friendship circle, I had met many gay men and hoped that some contacts could lead me to still others, but who was I looking for? What would an individual with a positive gay identity look like? There is no "test" that can determine this.

My intuition led me to individuals who were articulate and who felt good about themselves as gay men. This didn't mean that they had to have it "all worked out." No one knows what that would look like! In total, I interviewed fifteen gay men and one gay adolescent, ranging in age from sixteen to sixty-one.

All of the interviews were taped and transcribed verbatim. In writing the stories contained in this book, I worked from the transcripts themselves, retaining the co-researcher's own words wherever possible. Consequently, each co-researcher has, for the most part, told his own story in his own words.

Some details have been changed, however, to protect

confidentiality. All names have been changed and other details that might identify the co-researchers or others mentioned. These changes include locations (such as birthplaces and other places cited), dates of events (other than historical dates), and ages.

A researcher also needs to extract important themes contained in the stories. Through a systematic, time-consuming process called *coding*,[10] each transcript is carefully reviewed.

Structuring the Stories

Broadly speaking, positive gay men go through three phases of identity development: before they come out to themselves, while they are coming out, and during their establishment of a positive gay identity. The main sections of this book follow this same structure: (1) *Before Coming Out*; (2) *Coming Out* (i.e., self-identification as gay); and (3) *Beyond Coming Out*.

It was difficult, and somewhat imprecise, to break down each co-researcher's story into these three parts. There is often some overlap between the phases. The breaking of each story into three parts, however, establishes important milestones in the lives of gay men. Not all gay men go on to develop positive gay identities; and this is where *Beyond Coming Out* provides the reader insight into this crucial achievement.

A *Summary of Themes* derived from each phase of identity development immediately follows each of the major sections. These summaries draw the individual stories together, and they also provide the academic support for each theme.

Before my co-researchers are introduced and allowed to tell their stories, chapter one will help you understand the importance of this topic to me. It is my story.

Chapter One
Finally Out

Kevin, 43

I feel like Rip Van Winkle sometimes, like I'm just waking up. Things like crying—I find myself crying now. I had given it up when I was eight. Or laughing. Giggling. Roughhousing with my kids and having it be safe. Playing. Getting angry at somebody I love. Telling the truth. Feeling something in the moment it's actually happening, instead of five minutes later, five years later, always later. Taking risks I never would have taken before. Just kind of waking up. It's a silly metaphor, but it's what flowers do. They just come out.
(Bass & Davis, 1992, p. 168).

Before Coming Out

I remember playing with my friends when I was seven years old, enjoying their company outside on a warm summer day. We played tag, we chased each other, we wrestled, we laughed. I liked them, and they liked me. Nothing about it seemed remarkable.

Mom didn't like it, though. I could see the expression on her face through the window: a scowl that made Halloween ghouls seem friendly by comparison. She had told me before that I should play with other boys, not with girls. I didn't understand why. I thought I should be able to choose my own friends. Deep down, I knew that it was a sissy thing to do, to play with girls, but they were my friends. Nonetheless, I just wanted to be like the other kids. I didn't want to be different.

I caused an uproar between my parents when I asked them for a doll. My sisters had dolls, but they often excluded me from their play. I wanted one of my own. My parents worried that if they gave me a doll, it might hurt me in some deep way. I eventually got my wish, although I didn't think either of them were happy about it, but I really liked my doll.

I've had a deep fear of water from a very young age. My dad once called me a sissy because I would not wade further than ankle deep. I hated that word, *sissy*, especially when Dad used it. I knew he was disappointed in me. I just wanted to be like the other kids. I didn't want to be different.

I began to develop erotic feelings toward a male when I was ten years old. I adored my future brother-in-law's body. He was nineteen and nicely developed everywhere. I remember being at the beach that same summer, cautiously staring at an incredibly handsome teenager. His tanned, shirtless torso shone under the dimming light of dusk. The evening's coolness accentuated his perfect pectorals and erect nipples. I was nearly breathless with arousal. I wanted to replace his girlfriend and be the one he embraced.

I also wanted to sink into the earth and never re-emerge. What was wrong with me? I didn't want to be like this. There was a word for people like this, and I was not going to be one of them.

Around age twelve, I saw two young teens doubling on a bike. They were both blonde, blue-eyed stallions. Both were handsome, wearing blue jeans and open jean jackets, shirtless underneath. I found myself fixated again, staring at their indescribable beauty. They noticed my stare and rudely yelled, *"Take a picture, it will last longer, faggot!"* This was the first time I had been called that name. I knew what it meant, and it was the worst thing you could call a guy. My feelings were hurt, and I didn't ever want to hear that vile word again. I still just wanted to be like the other kids. I didn't want to be different...but I was well on my way.

I had my first crush on an agemate at age thirteen. He had been in my grade seven class. I thought he was incredibly cool, and gorgeous. He reminded me of Donny Osmond, whom I also thought was beyond mortal description. At the end of grade seven, he expressed interest in hanging out with me when all of his "cool" friends were away for the summer. I couldn't believe it. I was so uncool it hurt. I wore welfare glasses, I owned an interesting array of "flood" pants, and I looked and acted like a total nerd. I tried hard to suppress my deepest feelings so that I would fit in, yet I never did. This fostered a deep sense of insecurity and low self-esteem within me, which would remain for years to come.

That summer, 1971, was my best teenage summer. I adored my friend, and he could do no wrong in my eyes. We hung out together daily. When school began, however, he treated me like I no longer existed. I felt crushed, but I had known this summer thing would end. I was merely a fill-in. We were never physical, but my feelings for him were very strong. Although I hurt deeply, I could not let anyone know about my pain. They would think I was a fag.

I began dating women at age eighteen. Losing my virginity was an interesting experience, one that I subsequently analyzed for a long time. There was no question regarding the pleasure of orgasm. It increased my desire to have a girlfriend for both companionship and sex, but I found it difficult to establish. Most women I dated only want to be friends. I was convinced I was ugly and unlovable.

At age twenty, I met a seventeen-year-old I will call Dana. We started dating and soon became intimate. She was attractive, and I visited her three times a week, primarily for sex. We also did things out of the bedroom, but my head pointed mostly in one direction. After eight months of this, I felt guilty. The realization had been building that I had virtually no feelings for Dana, and it came as no surprise when I broke up with her. I never grieved over her, but I often grieved over how I unwittingly used her.

I wondered if I would ever fall in love. I romanticized the thought of being in love, but I seriously doubted that it would ever happen to me. Why was I not worthy? I didn't understand the messages I was giving myself. Little did I know what would soon transpire.

At twenty-two years of age, I began my second job after earning a bachelor of arts degree, working at a detention facility for delinquent youth. These adolescents really liked me, and I responded well to them. I respected them, and I enjoyed joking around with them. Sometimes I thought I was right where they were. Deep down, I had always felt like a deviant. I didn't know why. I thought it helped me relate to the underdog, though, and so perhaps it was a blessing.

I liked to spend a lot of time talking to a sixteen-year-old named Roger. It was like I tucked him in at night; I sat on the edge of his bed, and we talked. We related well to each other. He was dreadfully handsome and well-built for his age. His muscles allured me. Soon he returned home, and I suspected that I would never see him again, but I felt good because I thought I had got through to him.

We wrote letters to each other, and I enjoyed having a pen pal. A few months later, he was in crisis with his parents, and he called to ask if he could stay with me at my mom's. Mom agreed to have him stay with us for two weeks, but as two weeks metamorphosed into six, and as his reckless lifestyle clashed with Mom's, she could take no more. Roger had to go and, surprisingly, so did I. I moved away for the first time with a sixteen-year-old, and my mom's intuition was sharp that day. She asked, with a quivering voice strangely ready to break, "*Are you a homosexual?*"

Are you a homosexual? Imagine my own mother asking me this! I had been insulted before, but my mom ought to have known better. I reassured her that it was merely time I moved out. Mom was insightful, but even she couldn't have foreseen the devastation that would soon follow.

Roger saw me as his best friend, and of course I was. I would have done anything for him. His lifestyle was considerably different from mine, though. We often smoked marijuana together, and that aroused feelings in me I couldn't, or wouldn't, understand. Meanwhile, he brought young women over almost every night, and I didn't understand why I was going through emotional hell, tortured by bedroom sounds I heard through paper-thin walls.

A few months later, I could no longer function. I didn't know what was wrong with me. I felt confused, unmotivated, irrational, and anxious. One night I experienced a severe panic attack and I was hospitalized. The psychiatrist told me that my stepfather had said he thought I might be a homosexual. I felt such disgust that anyone, especially my family, would think this of me. A few days later, I left the hospital and moved into a Christian center for people suffering emotional distress. Thankfully, I had already had several sessions with Hans, the resident Christian counselor, before becoming an occupant there myself.

I enjoyed our counseling sessions. We talked about my natural father's death, and I grieved for this. Each session, I grieved some more, yet I continued to get worse. Soon I could only get out of bed to wash and to eat. My sleep was fitful, and sometimes I awakened in a delirious state. I would bang the wall. I was sure I had lost my mind, and I didn't know why.

Hans and I never talked about what was causing my pain.

Somehow, I could never utter that I felt completely heartbroken, and he could never ask. I didn't have a vocabulary for that gnawing pain, so I kept on hurting for months, adhering to a code of silence that perhaps only the military would commend.

Eventually a new day was born. The sun shone brightly that day, and I could see the color of light again. The greying of my heart had lifted, and I knew then that Hans had been incorrect in believing my pain was about my father's death. I then understood what daily marijuana use could do to a young man's mind. It could twist your feelings all around and make you believe things that were not true. I believed that this was the source of my problems and vowed never to smoke it again.

Dating women occurred sporadically, and unsuccessfully. I was not bonding to any of them, and neither were they to me. Years of loneliness blurred my hope. Perhaps another degree would help, I thought.

Within two months of beginning university, I met June. The first night I met her, we went to her place to have tea. She was such an intellectual, and I was impressed.

We began dating, and I developed a respect for her like I had never felt toward a woman. Our talks delved into every possible dream and reality that words could describe. Was this love? I reticently thought so. We moved in together, and before the federal government took away a matrimonial tax advantage, I proposed to her. She accepted. Our friendship grew ever stronger, and we loved spending time together. We walked, we talked, we dined, we played.

And then there was sex. I tried to analyze it, but I was so far away. I fantasized about men mostly, and sometimes about women. The pleasure of orgasm was significant to me, but I could not understand why June did not enjoy having sex with me. I cared for her deeply. Our caring eventually blessed us with two children. They were too beautiful for words.

Nonetheless, strange things began happening to me. In fall 1992, my greatest pleasure was coming from getting to know two young men at the college where I work. One I taught, the other I counseled. Why did I miss Jason so much when he missed a class? Why did I long for having the next session with Travis? I even started playing basketball with Travis occasionally at lunch time. My professional boundaries were getting stretched, and so was my psyche.

I had everything going for me. I had children. I had a nice house. I succeeded at my job. I created a successful private practice. I taught. I mentored. I worked…and worked…and worked.

Yet I felt like I was going crazy, and I didn't know why. I yelled too often at my kids, I drank excessively, I had my own separate bedroom at home, my back was killing me from a disk that I had ruptured earlier, and my feelings for these two guys were beyond me. This attack of pain was excruciatingly severe, and it wasn't just my lower back anymore. I reached out for help.

My new psychiatrist was brilliant, insightful, and caring. He asked poignant questions that deeply frightened me, however. At the end of our first session, I felt like vomiting. I couldn't imagine having just shared such deep thoughts, feelings, and fantasies. He sent me away with some questionnaires to complete and asked that I return them before our next session.

Near the end of our second session, he told me that he knew what my underlying problem was. Funny how I felt so arrogant hearing him say that. How could he know my problem so quickly, when I have been unable to figure it out my entire life? I said to him, "Well, what is it?" Then I became aware of a deeper fear I wasn't expecting, as though I anticipated hearing that I had cancer or something equally terrifying. He looked at me, and replied, **"You are a homosexual, a gay man who has never come to terms with yourself."**

Coming Out

I was seeing this psychiatrist about my confusion and my unhappiness, and now my head was exploding. I felt overwhelmed with an array of feelings and emotions firing through my nervous system simultaneously. From fear, anxiety, distrust, anger, betrayal, guilt, shame, disappointment, confusion, shock, disbelief, and outrage on the one hand, to joy, exhilaration, certainty, trust, euphoria, mania, and knowing on the other. The yin and the yang in mortal combat, truth and lies in monumental karmic collision. Was this my brain on drugs? No, this was my brain facing reality.

I think drugs would have been easier. During the months of healing that followed, I became more emotional than ever before in my life. My thoughts and feelings were on a roller- coaster. I quit my private practice and stopped sessional teaching. I left what I could to embrace what I needed to face.

My sessions with the psychiatrist never got any easier either. He challenged my thinking, often in Socratic dialogue. His arguments were persuasive, and denial was giving way to something I had learned to ignore and devalue: my deepest, most passionate feelings.

I had now been seeing my therapist for six months. I decided to tell my wife everything one night in July 1993. We retired to the living room to talk, and I told her. Initially she displayed little adverse reaction—denial was not my domain only. We continued enjoying each other's company through the months of summer, although she was masking a deep depression, the extent of which neither of us recognized yet.

The two of us met my psychiatrist together for one session. He told us that we didn't have a marriage. We knew this already, but hearing it from him solidified the inevitability that our marriage would end.

I wrote a journal entry on November 8, 1993:

It seems that the reality of leaving June has hit me hard. She has gone out (9:30 p.m.), and I am going to bed (10:00 p.m.). Soon I will need to once again get used to this aloneness. I don't think I can walk out on June...I love her too much. Why would I leave her and the kids for the emptiness I feel? Gay guys seem so noncommittal—like fuck buddies. But I am getting older - 37 to be exact—and I feel the clock churning [stomach churning].

When June gets home, she lies with me. Tears flowing down my face, I can't talk to her yet. I need more time, I am so choked. I want to tell her how I feel, how scared I am, and I want her to understand. I don't want to hurt her...she is the closest I have to a soulmate. Can my soul be so wrong? Do I need to leave her and take up my own residence? I'm not sure I can cope with this...I'm really not sure. The fear of total incapacitating depression (I've been there before) lurks in my psyche. I don't know how I could cope with another bout. Am I bringing it on myself? Can I stop it without denying myself again?

Many questions plagued my mind. The transition from posturing as a straight man with a wife and two children to being a gay man became the most difficult change I had ever faced. More than anything, I valued having an intact family, and being there for them. I was throwing a boulder on the very value that I held dearest to my heart.

Where was my hope? I hated myself at times, and despised myself. My only hope was that I would someday find love. Maybe I would come to know what it is like to feel passion for someone, someone who could reciprocate.

I began dating men and entered a new phase of life. Robert was the first man I courted. We arrived back at his place in the late afternoon on a warm autumn day. Before leaving the car, I leaned over to kiss him on the lips. He backed off, noticeably uncomfortable. I realized that in the past, I had never hesitated to kiss my date in public before. Now I had entered a different world.

Once inside his dwelling, I continued my advance and experienced the roughness of a five o'clock shadow for the first time. It hurt my sensitive skin, and later my chest was raw from the facial abrasiveness. I left wondering how many women have experienced similar skin irritation. I also wondered why I had to go through this.

There were many changes. I went to a gay rodeo, and guys were dancing two-step together. I had never seen anything like it. My own fear grew as my friend John asked me to dance. Following his encouragement, I succumbed, but I felt horrified. I managed to overcome the initial trauma, but it still looked and felt odd to me.

Our house was for sale, but there were no offers. House prices had dropped, and ours was apparently overpriced. I still felt ambivalence about being gay, and I still struggled with how I felt about leaving June. Then I met Darren.

Darren was a chiropractor, and a potentially hot catch. He taught me so much about what it meant to be gay. One day we shopped for new clothes and created a new look for me. The outside, however, was nothing compared to what was happening to me inside. I hadn't felt that passionately for someone since I was twenty-two. I thought I loved Darren, and it seemed that Darren was beginning to love me, when he announced that he would be moving to Vancouver in a few months. He was gone within a few weeks, and so was my heart.

June and I then priced the house to sell, and it sold quickly. I applied to four graduate schools, hoping to attend University of British Columbia in Vancouver to reacquaint myself with Darren.

That turned out to be false hope. Darren and I were finished, and my naiveté delayed my realizing it.

Beyond Coming Out

I am thankful that my spirit didn't let me sleep forever. Feelings are either faced, or they haunt you. Until there is a voice, there are no words to make sense of experience. My therapist helped me find a voice. At first it sounded like a scream, but even that was better than the sound of eternal silence.

For months following Darren's exodus, I dated several men, desperately seeking a life partner. Disillusionment permeated my heart as I came to doubt seriously if a sincere, committed relationship with a man was possible. When I least expected it, a man I had felt limerence for since meeting him a year earlier became dateable. Limerence transcended to love, and for the first time, I fell for a person who reciprocated. My life as a committed partner began again.

After coming out, most of the people I eventually disclosed to were shocked, although two people who knew me well said that they had suspected it soon after meeting me years earlier. Nonetheless, I assumed that if I wanted to, I could hide my orientation, and I wondered what it would feel like to be identified as gay. While attending the University of Alberta, I decided to find out. On June 21, 1996, a hair stylist dyed my hair platinum blonde. With a Caesar haircut, an earring and flamboyant clothing at my age, I decided that I had developed the closest to a stereotypical "gay look" that was possible for me. The most significant event occurred days later, on Canada Day, while I was at Sylvan Lake, Alberta, walking down the beach with my partner:

> *Journal entry, July 1, 1996:*
> *Lots of looks, smirks, stares, laughter, whispers—no one to my face, however. Lots of macho-looking redneck guys here today. (Later at night while in a tent) My partner and I overhear teens kicking a ball outside our tent. The first male says emphatically, "Watch where you kick the ball—that's where the fags are!" The second male says, shushing the first, "They're there, you know." The female teenager then speaks up and says, "Do you guys have a*

problem with that?" After my partner falls asleep, I cry. The hurt is not just for me, but for others who have had to endure this and much worse.

I had more questions after this. I wondered, "How will strangers react if I tell them?" I took a class that summer and when my turn came to give the thought for the day, I disclosed to the entire class of fourteen women and two men. I felt really nervous and it was hard. After my disclosure, we spend a fair amount of time discussing it. One woman broke into tears as she empathized with me. Others shared some very positive feedback.

It was mostly an uneventful summer. I think Canadians generally leave one another alone, or maybe it's a result of my age, but aside from hearing a few people call me a *faggot* under their breath, the only other significant memory was when I went hiking by myself in the Canadian Rockies. It is customary practice to greet others whom you meet while on a hiking trail. As I approached an older couple, I greeted them and smiled. Both ignored me completely and kept walking as though I didn't exist.

In retrospect, I think it was far more difficult for me *before* I came out. Then, I used to ignore myself, and that seemed far more distressing. By age thirty-nine, I don't think I really cared what anyone thought. After all, what else did I have to lose?

None of this was easy, however, and I still struggle. My most recent challenge concerns my children. They continue to receive indoctrination from our society about gay people, and much of this is still tainted with false stereotypes and misguided messages that wrongly suggest our inferiority. They also attend Catholic grade school. When my daughter innocently asked me during a dinner party "Daddy, are you gay?" and I responded, "Yes, dear, we have talked about that before," she replied with a tone of astonishment, "But Daddy, I *hate* gays!" Needless to say, this was not a great thing to hear, especially since every adult at the dinner party was a gay person. My children are victims of conditioning, and I can only do so much to correct the damage.

Of course, my children don't know everything I have experienced. They are still young and easily influenced by others. I have an obligation to teach them wisely. Being a gay father is the toughest role

I now face. Thank God I have the courage to face it. I am no more and no less than I always was. I am OUT, and I am proud.

Upon reflection, I think love developed when I was ready to give it fully. Throughout my life, I had held back from expressing my deepest tenderness toward another—the other being a male. So often, I had felt like a person without a soul. The greatest part of me, my unobstructed ability to love another person fully, was now released from the nameless prison. My emotions were no longer serving hard time. My escape had given me a passion and a zest for life which I had never experienced earlier.

Denying love and sexual attraction diminishes the artistry and passion in life. My enjoyment of the arts has increased since I came out. Before then, I did not enjoy ballet, the philharmonic, or most live theater. Beyond love, much of my sensitivity was repressed as well. I had found it hard to experience genuine empathy.

Thank God I finally have the chance to live my life with integrity. I have often wondered if there is anything more important than this. Being true to oneself is the lesson I most want to teach my children. I think I finally know how. I believe that as adults, we are deeply crippled if we do not have a strong sense of our own identity, and a love of what we see when we look in the mirror.

Chapter Two
The Co-Researchers

As mentioned earlier, I interviewed fifteen gay male adults and one gay adolescent. These people became the co-researchers. In this chapter, I will introduce each of them to you briefly. Because I was studying positive gay identity, and I knew no psychological test could measure this, I asked each co-researcher to write out their own definition of *positive gay identity*. Everyone provided a definition, except Alex. Alex was less committed to this project than the others, but his story nonetheless provides important insights into what it means, and doesn't mean, to have developed a positive gay identity.

1. Matthew, Age 32 - Retail Manager

A strong Mennonite upbringing led Matthew to begin pursuing his dream of becoming a minister. Homosexual dreams, however, began to change all that. Matthew's story provides a poignant example of how religious indoctrination does not, and cannot, prevent the development of a same-gender sexual orientation.

Matthew's Definition of "Positive Gay Identity": For me this would have to do with my feeling of accepting myself as gay (not wishing I were anything other than I am) as well as feeling a worthy member of society.

2. Peter, Age 40 - Legal and Business Consultant

After a pedophile molested him when he was nine years old, Peter began equating this man's behavior with his conception of homosexuality. His stereotypes and feelings toward another male waited in darkness until Peter's behavior became erratic and unconsciously suicidal. A therapist helped open his eyes to what was really occurring within him.

Peter's Definition of "Positive Gay Identity": Sense of self-acceptance, sense of pride, the absence of shame for being gay. Being unapologetic for one's gayness. Knowing that you can do anything you want to do. Being free of stereotypes.

3. Frank, Age 38 - Accountant

After finishing university, Frank and a group of fellow graduates celebrated by taking a trip to Florida. While partying at a straight bar, he noticed a poster advertising a big event at a local gay night club. Mixed feelings swelled inside when he arrived at the club's doorstep. Frank's experience there began his coming out.

Frank's Definition of "Positive Gay Identity": Personal comfort in disclosing your homosexuality to everyone you encounter, pride in yourself as being a good person, and an ability to act as an ambassador and advocate for gay acceptance within your sphere of influence.

4. Gavin, Age 32 - Businessman

Gavin came from a wealthy family and attended the best schools. Blessed with an upbringing that encouraged taking leadership, Gavin became the manager of two adjoining gay bars at age nineteen. He strongly believes that he is successful today because of his sexual orientation.

Gavin's Definition of "Positive Gay Identity": Instead of providing a definition, Gavin handed me an article and explained that it summarized for him the meaning of positive gay identity. The author is Armistead Maupin and the article is called "Design for Living". His "blueprint for a more fulfilling life" includes the following advice: (1) Stop begging for acceptance, (2) Don't run away from straight people, (3) Refuse to cooperate in the lie, (4) Stir up some shit now and then, (5) Don't sell your soul to the gay commercial culture, (6) Stop insulting the people who love you by assuming they don't know you're gay, and (7) Learn to feel mortal.

5. Jonathan, Age 30 - Systems Analyst

Jonathan was born in Hong Kong and raised in Canada by traditional Chinese parents. His story recounts how he overcame the conflicts resulting from being Chinese and gay.

Jonathan's Definition of "Positive Gay Identity": Being able to carry out a gay lifestyle on a daily basis with dignity and pride.

6. Jerome, Age 48 - Politician

Jerome's life was relatively uneventful until the fateful night he became the victim of a police raid at a bathhouse. When the media searched for individuals to interview, Jerome stepped forward and unintentionally gave his real name. Going public changed Jerome's life significantly, and unexpectedly.

Jerome's Definition of "Positive Gay Identity": Living in the world as a male whose sexuality is gay and using my gay identity as an opportunity and an asset.

7. Fréderic, Age 38 - School Teacher and Artist

Fréderic didn't have an easy life. His brother sexually abused him in childhood, which led to long-term sexual difficulties. He later became HIV positive, which made him as he put it, two kinds of gay positive. His story is an inspiration to everyone who lives with a chronic illness.

Fréderic's Definition of "Positive Gay Identity": To be able to integrate one's gayness in one's daily life. To be proud and rooted spiritually and emotionally as a gay person.

8. Tommy, Age 41 - Sales and Marketing Representative

Tommy came out in second-year university, and he and two other students began the school's first gay organization. As they put up posters announcing the club, an altercation erupted. He also began the first gay tabloid in his city.

Tommy's Definition of "Positive Gay Identity": Acceptance of homosexuality as a legitimate sexual orientation. Belief that homosexuality enriches life in a unique way. Appreciating the unique influence that homosexuality has on life experience.

9. Cliff, Age 30 - Entertainer and Bartender

Knowing he was gay from a young age, Cliff lept at the opportunity to live with a young gay couple for three years when he was a teenager. He describes his experience of becoming a renowned drag queen, along with his perspective of the drag queen subculture.

Cliff's Definition of "Positive Gay Identity": Being a friendly, positive influence on friends and people I have met, having an open mind and a weird sense of humor.

10. Paul, Age 50 - Retired Retailer

Nearing desperation and a likely suicide, Paul surrendered married life with children for a chance to become authentic. A highlight of Paul's story is his love for Roger, his partner of eleven years.

Paul's Definition of "Positive Gay Identity": Loving   yourself enough to accept yourself for who you really are and not letting other people influence you. Being able to live your life as a gay person with no regrets.

11. John, Age 61 - Lawyer

John's family was part of the upper echelon of society, and as expected, he became a respected lawyer and cherished husband and father. Unexpectedly, he became unable to continue hiding his true feelings. Later, suffering a severe gay bashing and seeing this minimized by the police sparked a significant aspiration within him.

John's Definition of "Positive Gay Identity": The description that applies to a gay male who is comfortable with his sexual orientation.

12. David, Age 16 - Junior High School Student

Like most gay adolescents, David struggled to find acceptance by his peers. He also struggled to be heard and understood through his often garbled words, and not to be pitied for his uncontrolled motor movements. Cerebral palsy has not silenced David, however, as evidenced by his story.

David's Definition of "Positive Gay Identity": I think a positive gay identity is that in which I can feel comfortable about myself and who I am.

13. Glenn, Age 46 - Government Administrator

Glenn was slow in developing his sexuality. Frequent trips to England, however, led to his coming out as a leatherman. Glenn shares valuable insights, revealing a behind-the-scenes look at leather subculture.

Glenn's Definition of "Positive Gay Identity": A positive gay identity means that one's sexual orientation has integrated itself as part of the whole being, no more or no less important than every other aspect of that which is "me."

14. Troy, Age 24 - University Student

Troy felt different from the time he was three years old. Apart from having to overcome stereotypes, Troy's coming out was uneventful. His story is an example of a young person who came to accept his feelings, without fearing serious consequences.

Troy's Definition of "Positive Gay Identity": At peace with oneself. Striving to be "out" to as many people as possible (i.e., close relationships). Supportive of all struggling (disadvantaged, minority, oppressed groups). Working with the majority, not against it. Politically active—working for better days ahead.

15. Andrew, Age 29 - Education Coordinator

Andrew's sister came out, and helped set the stage for his debut a few years later. To break through his own fears about being gay, Andrew became a bartender in a gay bar while attending law school. Andrew is very "out," and his story speaks about the resulting sacrifices.

Andrew's Definition of "Positive Gay Identity": Positive gay identity for me begins with self-identification as a gay man or lesbian. Increasingly, there is an awareness, understanding, and reconciliation with the world in which we live, the way we are socialized, and the way it affects our lives. This does not necessarily mean "out," but by necessity means a willingness to see, and work with, our own homophobia.

16. Alex, Age 23 - Executive Director

Alex is an Aboriginal, adopted and raised by dysfunctional Caucasian parents. His adolescence was marred by drug abuse, trafficking, and prostitution. Today he holds the top position in an agency that works with troubled youth.

Alex's Definition of "Positive Gay Identity": (None provided).

Chapter Three
Before Coming Out Stories

Matthew, 32

I was born in the province of Saskatchewan. My father is a retired vice principal and teacher. My mother stayed home to raise me, my two elder sisters, and my younger brother. Religion was an integral part of my life. I grew up in the Mennonite Brethren faith, which is considered evangelical and fundamentalist. I will come back to its effect on my coming out later.

I first became aware that I might be gay when I was very young, between ages six and eight. However, because I've come through a very religious background, that was always greatly suppressed. That was not something talked about, and homosexuality was always viewed in my family as negative.

We moved into a new neighborhood when I was seven. Nearby lived two brothers. The older boy, Bert, paid a lot of attention to my brother and me. We did all kinds of deviant things, like picking up butts in the alley and going through people's garbage and picking up their porno magazines. He had a fort beside his house, and we would go in there and do stuff. We would look at these magazines and do all the things we weren't supposed to do. Bert was entering puberty and he showed us his penis. I remember thinking, "Oh my God, that thing is so huge!" It was impressive, but I was actually more attracted to his brother.

I remember being attracted to older boys or the good-looking boys in my class, mostly because I wanted them to notice me so I would feel a part of their group. They were always athletic, and I wasn't. I was pretty innocent. That didn't stop the feelings of guilt, however.

I remember being in the locker room after gym in grade six, and someone called me a fag or something like that. I was devastated. I took that really personally, and I hated that feeling. Those sorts of words always bothered me. I was really sensitive to that...perhaps overly sensitive.

In high school, I didn't know what to do with my sexual desires.

I was confused. I didn't even masturbate. I tried to convince myself that I was well disciplined and that's why I didn't have desires for women. In my church, sex before marriage was not considered an option, and it just was not practiced. I believed everything the church had to say.

I dated girls because I thought I was supposed to, but it never got past a closed-mouth kiss. Nothing ever lasted long, and none of my dates were significant to me. There were girls that attracted me, but I was attracted to them more emotionally than physically.

There was definitely a reaction toward certain men, however, especially men dressed in leather. Seeing them gave me a hard-on, and I felt guilty about that. I also felt deviant because I would sometimes watch them or follow them. I remember trying to time my walk home because a certain guy walked the same path.

Many of my earliest fantasies about men had to do with leather and bondage. I fantasized about tactile sensations: the feeling of the leather, the smell, and the man inside the leather. I remember being really turned on by an episode of *BJ and the Bear* where BJ was tied up while wearing a leather jacket.

In grade twelve, there was a group of us that went into this thing called a swing choir. I became particularly good friends with Daryl and John. The year after high school, Daryl came out of the closet. I suspected that John was also gay, but he has never come out. I remember there was a bond or connection between Daryl and me, but we never discussed it. Instead, we both dated girls. We were not admitting to ourselves yet.

After high school, I attended Bible school for two years. I lived in a dorm, and I remember really worrying as my gay awareness grew. One of my first classes in Bible school was called "Ethics. "It was obviously at the forefront of my mind, because I did a paper on homosexuality. My feelings concerned me.

Between my first and second year of Bible school, I went to Germany for ten weeks on a mission. That summer was the first time I met people who had been brought up in other faiths. For the first time, I put a face to different religions and I asked myself, "Why am I right? Why do I believe this?" Simply because I was brought up believing it. I think that was the first glimpse of doubt I had about my faith.

In second year, I wrote in a journal about my attraction to certain guys in the dorm. I was suffering from much guilt and fear. My fears were of (1) being sent to hell or being an evil person, (2) not being able to have a family, (3) being ridiculed if anyone knew what I was feeling, (4) losing my family, and (5) entering the gay life as I perceived it then. The stereotype I had was vivid: a bunch of really flamboyant, effeminate perverts having thousands of sexual partners. This image insulted my moral code. Beyond morality, I was not attracted to that effeminate image either. My attractions were toward really masculine men.

I was concerned, so I spoke to a prof about it. He said this is just a phase many men go through and that I shouldn't worry about it. As I was already dating women, I thought my same-sex attraction would disappear if I fell in love. I dated Anne seriously at that point, and we had fun together. I was really attracted to her because although she was not really physically attractive to me, she had an outrageous sense of humor. At that point in my life I was intending to become a minister, and she was also a committed Mennonite Brethren. Although we got along well, it didn't work out.

After Bible school, I attended university with a major in drama. Although there were some gay people, none of us were out, or open, about our homosexuality. We were introduced to gay writers, however. There were several gay plays produced while I attended university, and I often got cast in gay roles. For example, I remember being cast as a young lover of a man in second year. I didn't want the part at all, but eventually I decided if I was going to be an actor, I would have to open myself up to many roles, so I did it and received a lot of recognition for it. My part was a really touching scene that many people looked at as a highlight of the play. The head of the department was impressed by my performance and said I would make a very nice gay boy, or something to that effect, to the director. After that, more parts came my way that were gay-related or contained gay characters.

I felt somewhat alienated from the others at the university, however, and I attributed this to the fact that I was religious. I always thought I didn't completely fit in with these people because I didn't drink, I didn't smoke, and I didn't swear. In retrospect, I think I felt alienated because I was in the closet.

Occasionally I would wake from sleep after having very erotic dreams. I remember one dream in which I was French-kissing this guy passionately, and he reciprocated. It continued, and I had anal intercourse with him, but when he began to do the same to me, I woke immediately. Although it felt totally gross in the dream, when I awakened I discovered I had had a wet dream. I kept praying aloud, asking, "What is going on?" My religious beliefs and my homosexuality were in dire conflict. The conflict didn't stop the multitude of homosexual thoughts, dreams, and fantasies, however. They continued unabated.

Peter, 40

I had a big aversion to homosexuality growing up. When I was nine years old, I was in the showers at a public swimming pool and an old creepy man began molesting me. He wore coke bottle glasses, a wrinkled raincoat, and looked like the stereotype of a pedophile. He stuck his hands down my swimming trunks. I told the lifeguard, who then phoned the police. I was incredibly traumatized, not only by the incident, but by the justice system. I was a witness for the prosecution, and I had to describe in intimate, humiliating detail this whole incident. I also had to describe my body parts. In those days they did not clear out courtrooms for child molestation charges. There were kids my own age in the courtroom, watching for the sheer entertainment, as it was the traditional defense of the day to suggest that the kid was lying. The man was acquitted because there were no witnesses to the incident. I felt humiliated and degraded in a public forum. As a lawyer today, I realize it was an evidentiary acquittal and not because I wasn't believed, but nobody told me that at the time. It was one of the most traumatic experiences of my life, and at the end I felt I had lost because nobody believed me.

Why I am telling you about this event is that the term pedophile was never used. It had always been ingrained in me that this horrible, evil man that violated me was a gay man, a homosexual, a fag, an old queer. I remember all the terms used. I had been "fruited up." There was no distinction made back then that this man was a pedophile, and even my mother told me that this is what queer people do.

In retrospect, I realize I had homoerotic feelings when I was twelve or thirteen years old. For example, I used to be a competitive swimmer. My favorite part of competitive swimming was the locker rooms, where all the boys were changing afterwards. All these little naked wieners flopping around were exciting to watch, but it was nothing that I identified as sexual or homoerotic. After I came out, I reviewed my memory of these early sensations, and I now understand that I was sexually excited. The human mind's ability to deny still surprises me. I had contorted logic and somehow rationalized that these feelings I had were not homoerotic. That, after all, would have insinuated that I was a fag.

I remember being in a hot spring with my grandfather. We were in the changing room, and I saw boys that were older than I was—fifteen, sixteen—and they were naked. I remember getting very excited about this. It scared the hell out of me, because people had told me that after having been molested by this old man, it would be a real struggle to make sure that I didn't turn out like he did. It was believed that if you were molested by an older queer, you'd grow up to be queer.

I also remember finding a *Playboy* in Dad's den. One issue had a movie review in it, and there were photos of women removing a guy's clothes. It was the only picture of a male penis that I had seen in *Playboy*. That edition of the magazine gave me hours of pleasure. I would go off masturbating to my little heart's content in some cubbyhole in our house, but I would not have acknowledged that that particular issue of *Playboy* excited me so much because it had the scene with the naked man in it.

My family of origin was very dysfunctional. My mother was and still is severely mentally ill, and my family goes to great efforts to make my mother appear normal to the outside world. We would love to portray this picture of the Walton family to everyone, but my mother's sadism and cruelty were really extraordinary. She knows I have a fatal allergy to peanuts, but since I was a little kid, and to this day, she offers me peanuts and peanut butter baking; she has been trying to kill me since childhood. I was very fond of my hamsters, and she would kill them to taunt and ridicule me. She always waited until I got attached to something before taking it away. She still hates me. I go there and it's still crazy-making.

I saw little of my father when I was very young. He was a printer then and would often sleep at the shop. I think he did it partly to get away from my mom. In a weak moment only a few years ago, he cried one day and admitted that he never understood why mother hated me so much.

I left home at the age of sixteen, and I would have become a street kid if I had been less smart. I found acceptable ways to be out in the streets. I got money through government programs and scholarships and things, instead of stealing or working on the streets. I became very well educated. I earned a BA in political science, two law degrees, and fulfilled most of the requirements for an MA in political science.

I married when I was twenty-one years old, after a long engagement. Jane visited me in London while I worked on my first law degree. We married, she returned to Canada after ten days, and I didn't see her for another two years. It seemed like a perfect arrangement. When I got home, it became more problematic, although I was able to perform heterosexually. We had twelve years together, and I felt increasingly unable to continue.

I never remember fantasizing about Jane's breasts or her vagina or anything like that. Did I like feeling her breasts? I could have shaken her hand and gotten the same jollies out of it. Did I like going down on her? No thank you, I didn't really like it much at all, but it sure made her squeal, and that made me happy. The physical responses and emotional responses from Jane are what turned me on.

I became an owner of a popular gay bar around 1987. I tried to make the gay club a clean, drug-free, abuse-free type of place. The patrons, however, didn't want that. They liked the drugs, the poppers, and all the rest of it. This was part of the scene. I realized the place was unhealthy, and I didn't want to be a part of it. I gave ownership of the bar to the general manager in 1992. I said it's yours, and I walked away.

Owning the club and trying to make it a healthy place was probably about the worst thing I could have done to start my coming out, but it was the only place I knew that gay people congregated. Who did I meet at the club? I met the *nellie*[11] drag queens, the leather queens, the drug abusers, the drunks and the promiscuous types. I understood intellectually that gay people were not wrinkled old men with coke bottle glasses who molested little boys, but I didn't feel it yet in my heart. I met just about every possible negative stereotype of gays—people that hung around toilets, people that went to the baths and participated in frequent self-destructive activities.

Let me clarify that I don't believe that being effeminate is a bad thing and nor do I believe that people who go to baths, clubs, or toilets are "bad" either. Rather, I believe it is damaging to be unauthentic and to engage in self-destructive acts. Consequently, I think it is hurtful to act effeminately if you think you *should* act that way, rather than because it's who you *are*. At the time, I even sporadically entertained the idea that maybe that's what I had to become. The only thing that saved me from going into that life is that because I was so afraid of being gay in the first place, I just decided to shut everything down.

The difference between my feelings for men and women really hit me while I was still married. I remember a scene from a movie I saw when I was a little kid, where a little girl asked her mom, "How do I know when I'm in love?" Mom replied, "Oh honey, believe me, you'll know. You won't be able to eat, you won't be able to sleep, you'll think of nothing else but that person." And then the young teenage girl said, "Well then, I think I'm in love." That image has stuck with me for my whole life. I remember Jane and me discussing this scene from the movie and agreeing that it was a crock, because neither of us had any recollection of feeling that way when we "fell in love."

Then one year I met Bob, and we fell in love. And I couldn't eat and I couldn't sleep and I couldn't think of anything else but wanting to be with him. For the first time in my life I really felt head over heels, passionately in love. Every waking moment was spent thinking about Bob, and he felt the same about me. I finally realized that old movie didn't mislead us. That *is* how you feel when you fall in love. And I finally realized that I never had really fallen in love. I thought I had, because I was fond of Jane and she was a woman—therefore this must be love. But when I really fell in love with someone, I thought, "Oh my God!"

I started fantasizing about Bob every time I masturbated or had sex with Jane. I woke up in the morning with a smile on my face, thinking of Bob. I went to sleep with a smile on my face, thinking of Bob. Sexual relations with my wife became irritating, because it distracted me from what I really wanted to contemplate.

The critical point occurred when I was around thirty years old. I would just sit in my room and sob for no reason at all. There were many emotions that were trying to get out, and I couldn't identify the cause. I would chastise myself for feeling unhappy, because to everyone else I had reached the pinnacle of success in my career. Everything that everyone else thought would be a good thing to have, I had already achieved. I wasn't just a lawyer, I was the highest-ranking lawyer in the province. I held a judicial type position within the legislature.

Eventually, I was in such pain that I unwittingly began doing self-destructive things. I realized I was trying to kill myself when, for the fifth time in a month, I saw a red light and just continued driving on, seeing it as green in my mind, knowing it was red but seeing it as green. It was like the movies where everybody just barely misses one another by an inch. I would stop and say "I knew that light was red, so why did my mind interpret it as green?"

I remember occasions where I would take my asthma pills in the morning, and later realize that I had already taken my required dose five times earlier, not remembering each time that I had done so. I realized I was doing some strange things, and I wondered why. In retrospect, I realize I was trying to kill myself, but I certainly didn't dream of doing such a thing at a conscious level.

I was very much in love with Bob, without acknowledging that it was a love feeling. Admittedly, Bob was one of the craziest people I had ever met. He was a strong Mormon who was having trouble with his own sexuality. He had been in and out of youth detention centers and all that stuff. He had a hard time fitting into his family's idea of the good Mormon.

We both managed to contort reality and rationalize why we were both sucking each other's wieners for so long. I mean, this really wasn't *homosexuality*. Bob was and still is in denial. We managed to rationalize it wonderfully. This was just a guy thing, this was just a whatever. I don't know how many guys suck each other's wieners, but this was how much denial with which we were both quite adept, and we fed off each other. We affirmed that this really wasn't gay, this was just fooling around.

One night when I felt at the lowest depths of despair I called Bob to ask him if we could meet somewhere. I don't know why I called him, other than I felt he might have more experience feeling despair than anyone else I knew. I told Bob that I felt strange, and I started sobbing. He said, "You can't do this alone," and he recognized that I was taking the responsibility of the world on my shoulders. He suggested that I see his psychologist. Phoning him was the hardest call I ever made in my life, but I soon began the long psychotherapy process.

To build a positive gay identity, I had to go through a total break with my old life. I felt immensely unhappy, and I didn't know why. I was always an overachiever and I kept myself incredibly busy. I was running, running, running. In retrospect, I now know what I was running from.

Frank, 38

I was born in New Brunswick, but my family lived in Houston, Texas, during my first five years. My father, an alcoholic, was apparently drinking and hanging out at the press club there, and he was eventually transferred back to Saint John. I guess he was someone who slept around. My parents separated and divorced when I was twelve or thirteen years old.

My dad and I didn't have a good relationship. After my parents separated, my dad moved back to Texas. I would receive an annual Christmas gift from him, but there was no communication between us to any degree other than the odd letter. There was a period of about four or five years when I didn't hear from him at all. I felt that he had more interest in my sister. Although I can say that our relationship was probably fair until the separation, it was poor to bad afterwards.

My mother was the caregiver, the one who was always there for us. She would do the housework, the cooking, the nurturing, the health care, the whole nine yards. There's no better mother on the entire planet, that's how I feel. It's always been that way. When my parents separated, she was left with having to work at low-paying jobs. My grandparents were fairly well off and they were always there for us, however. I had good family support growing up.

I didn't respect my sister in my younger years because I felt she wasn't respecting my mother. We always had communication problems and probably more fights than average siblings. As time progressed, she became accepting of my being gay, and was proud to tell it to anybody she knew. She's actually been a positive support for me.

I attended a Catholic all-boys school during my elementary years. I started having feelings of being gay, or different, when I was quite young. Hockey and other sports did not interest me. My small group of friends enjoyed role-playing and acting out in other ways that were totally different from most of my peers.

I became aware of my attractions for males at around age sixteen. Magazines like *Penthouse* indicated that it was normal to have these feelings as a younger male and that there's nothing wrong with that. Consequently, I thought that this was just a stage or phase in my development.

I think I was uncomfortable with issues of sex. I also don't think I was in touch with my feelings. I was not aware of homoerotic feelings at all before age sixteen. I had some curiosity and I might play in the park with the boys, but I didn't experience sexual longing for a guy at that point.

My developing feelings for men were not directed toward television stars, actors, or passing strangers. It would always be with one of my close friends. For example, my erotic dreams would sometimes include this friend and create a situation where we were both naked together.

Somewhere between ages seventeen and nineteen, I became sexually active with women. I never slept around much, perhaps four women in total. I enjoyed the sex, but I still had ongoing desires or curiosities about men. At nineteen or twenty, I had my first homosexual experience. As time progressed, the feelings and thoughts I had for men intensified. As I started hanging out with gay friends, learning about the culture, and actually dating and being sexually intimate with men, I began identifying the feelings that I had over the past ten years.

I met Carol in grade eleven, and we dated for four years. I wouldn't say that I was head over heels in love with her. I was wondering how to get out of that relationship, because I didn't think she was someone I would marry.

I accepted a job opportunity in Europe, and while I was there, I had my first significant gay experience. I arrived in a town and asked a guy and a girl for directions to my hotel. A few minutes after leaving them, the same guy drove up in his car and offered me a ride. I said "Sure, that's great." After some preliminary conversation, he told me that the train station was a hang out for gay people. The next thing you know there's some touching and feeling going on and he's asking me if I want to go back to his place. I agreed, but as we're driving to his place, I'm thinking that I am going to be killed. It was a long drive, and we were getting further and further away from where I was supposed to be. I thought they'd never find me. This guy was a rugby player, and I wondered if maybe he was a basher. Obviously, that wasn't the case at all. Mostly, I felt excited.

This was the first time I had ever kissed a man and I felt very odd about it. It seemed so unusual. It took me a while to assimilate that and to say, "Okay, that wasn't so bad." The experience had no emotional meaning at all. It was an act, an illicit thing, I thought. Following the encounter, I didn't think much about the person at all.

The place I was billeted had a young man my age, and I thought he was interesting, but he had a girlfriend I was more interested in. I told him that I liked his girlfriend, and he said, "You can have her if you want." I accepted his generous offer, but it only amounted to some foolish touching between her and me.

I returned to university after the Europe trip. At this point Carol and I had broken up. I didn't date anybody or do anything for a year or so, after which I started dating another girl, Beth, who was in my class. We only had sex once, and that wasn't until a year and a half into our relationship. She was a virgin and had never had sex, but she wanted to try it, so she negotiated it with me. It was all rather formal. It wasn't completely satisfying, partly because she was nervous as hell.

While I was still seeing Beth, about twenty or thirty of us decided we were going to take a trip to Florida after we graduated, and we did. We would party on the beach and go out to the different clubs and drink beer and have a good time. There was a poster in a straight bar describing a big night at the Copa, which was a gay bar. I was interested in going, but Beth was down there with me. One night I hopped in a cab and arrived at this huge pink palatial place, and I told the cabbie that he had the wrong place. I was expecting some dark, seedy alley with all kinds of strange people around, but this was a well lit, beautiful building. He said, "This is the Copa."

The moment I walked in the door, it was like a dawning, a revelation. Here was this high energy place with a thousand gay men. It was a huge bar, and I really enjoyed myself. At this point I had never considered that there were that many more people like me. I had never really thought about being gay.

I found myself comfortable and really enjoying being in that environment. At that point I really had to start accepting many of the feelings that I had been having since age sixteen. When the night was over, I had an experience with one person I was interested in. We had sex, and I found that rewarding. Since I didn't go home that night, I had some stories to tell the next day to my roommates.

I felt guilty about the fact that I was still dating Beth. I ended up telling her what I had done the night before. She was immediately shocked and curious, "Like, what's going on with you?" The next night we went to the Copa together, and we had a good time. After we left, she said it was too much for her, and she felt it best if we didn't see one another. We broke up, and months later I discovered that she had been in a same-sex relationship.

After returning from Florida, I started working and going to the gay bar in Saint John. I was concerned about being identified there, and that made it uncomfortable for me to be gay in Saint John. At this point my family didn't know, my straight friends and school friends didn't know, and certainly people at work didn't know. I had no intention of letting them know either. I'm still like that to a degree, but I wish I could be more open with everybody that I encounter. It's one thing that will change for me over time.

Gavin, 32

The way I was raised and the family I grew up in provided me with some advantages. I come from a wealthy family. We always had the biggest house on the block and the best cars. It's very old wealth, and I was brought up much differently than my neighbors. Most of the kids that I grew up with were also fairly wealthy, but they were first generation wealth. There is a different dynamic in the way that works. For example, my friends had brand new skis every year or they went to Hawaii for Christmas. While they spent their money, I was told that we were penniless and that we couldn't afford all these things. If I wanted something like a new pair of skis, I was expected to buy them with my own money.

I realized when I was around eighteen that our family had a sizable amount of wealth. As a result, I was brought up in a position of leadership. I went to boarding school in Vancouver for my senior high school years and was trained to be a leader. I was chosen by the school as one of their star students for having future potential. I was sat down in the headmaster's office with the top masters of the school and given a lecture on what was expected of me. When you come from this type of family, you have responsibilities that you must attend to throughout your life. This is part of your upbringing and your birthright, I was told.

I had some attraction for males as far back as kindergarten. I remember sitting in this big room having milk and cookies. I noticed this other kid across the room who I just had to sit next to for no conscious reason. From grade six, I had crushes on certain guys in school. I assumed we were all the same, so when I was sitting in class watching somebody, I assumed that other guys had crushes on guys as well. I figured it was just something that was never discussed. These crushes were never sexual until I went to boarding school. I didn't suffer the name-calling through school that many of my present gay friends experienced. I was never teased, probably because I was neither wimpy nor effeminate.

When I was still quite young, my mother informed me that some men choose other men to love instead of women. She didn't say that was wrong or weird or anything like that; it was just a statement.

At boarding school I had a crush on a guy. I wanted to be his friend, I wanted to talk to him, I wanted to always be with him, and I wanted physical closeness. He was in a different residence house, and I knew that the only way I could see him fully naked was to be in that house. Although it was unheard of at the time, I was permitted to change residence. He graduated when I finished grade eleven.

His brother began grade ten at the same boarding school the subsequent year. I fell absolutely in love with him. I remember sitting on my bed thinking it would be really nice to see him naked, and then I fantasized about watching him masturbate. I even went to the extent of stealing this guy's pillows under the guise that they were fluffy and comfortable, but I wanted them because they contained his scent. The thought occurred to me, "Oh my God, I wonder if I'm gay." I remember having an image of some pansy dancing around, and I thought, "I am not like that." I managed to suffocate the sexual thoughts until I graduated.

There was a fellow who resided in the same house at the boarding school, who disclosed to me that he was gay. He took me to a couple of gay bars, which I enjoyed. I remember being in Edmonton for New Year's Eve that year, and we ended up in a gay bar. I had seen this attractive guy earlier in the evening and, when it came time for the New Year's kiss, I tried to find him. Everyone knew me there as straight, so when he saw me he hugged me, but he didn't kiss me. I was disappointed. The hug, however, gave me a really wonderful feeling. I got up about five o'clock the next morning and I walked all around Edmonton for about five or six hours thinking about the feeling that I had and how nice this hug felt. I tried to assess whether I might want to go further than that.

Jonathan, 30

I was born in Hong Kong, and my family moved to Canada when I was five. My father was concerned that my brother and I would lose our language and our culture, so he sent us back to Hong Kong six times or so to attend school. Sometimes my mother would miss us so much that we would return after a few months.

Religion never played a big part of my life. We were Catholic for a small period of time and that was only because I liked attending Sunday school. Spirituality to me is about finding inner peace.

I knew from a young age that I was different. I knew that I did not fit the norm in society, I knew that I would be ridiculed, and I knew that I probably would not give my parents children. At an early stage I said that this is going to be really tough, so I started looking at myself and wondering what I could do to keep myself happy instead of being depressed about not being like everybody else. During my final trip to Hong Kong at age twelve or thirteen, I told a close cousin that I'm very different and that I feel different. She was supportive. I started realizing that to feel good about myself, I needed to become honest with as many people as possible.

My parents always owned and operated restaurants, and I poured my first cup of coffee when I was nine. Customers thought I was the cutest thing. It was difficult for me when I met certain guys that turned me on. I remember just gawking at men from an early age. I didn't find kids attractive because I knew they were kids. I found late teenagers and men attractive. Perhaps that is where my attraction for older men developed.

I began experimenting with some friends when I was eleven or twelve. I recollect two experiences where we rubbed each other to orgasm. Both times were enjoyable. No other sexual experiences occurred for the next five years.

Jerome, 48

I grew up in a rather large family: three brothers and three sisters. We lived in a city of about fifty thousand people. In those days, I don't think I knew what gay was. The term was hardly ever used and there certainly wasn't anything about gays and about being homosexual on television. If there were any books on the subject, they were locked away in the library somewhere, and nobody talked about it. I don't think I was aware of what was going on in my own sexuality until I was sixteen or seventeen. It didn't seem to click the same way as with other people. As my siblings became involved with members of the opposite sex, I kept waiting for it to happen to me. It never did.

I remember an incident at a movie theater when I was sixteen or seventeen. While I was in the washroom stall, somebody next to me put his hand under my stall a couple of times. I had no idea what it meant, but it simultaneously terrified me and excited me. I think that particular incident made me realize that I found other men exciting, but I thought little about it at the time. As I thought about it over the next few weeks, however, I realized there was something fascinating about it.

Around the same age, I often went swimming in the summer. I remember being at the beach and spending more time looking at men than women. I found significant amounts of body hair exciting, a turn-on, without knowing why or being able to explain it. I needed some information and books to help me understand my feelings. I felt like I was in a wasteland. As I usually do in situations like that, I simply ignored my feelings. I had a couple of women as girlfriends back then, but it was very casual and nonsexual. We went to movies occasionally.

I don't think my family was aware that I was different from my brothers and sisters. I wasn't as athletic as two of my brothers, probably because I was always short. As time went on, I started running. Other than that, I soon dropped away from sports and became more involved in organizations and clubs. I was always encouraged to study, and I did fairly well academically.

Regarding my gayness, I remained totally unaware in high school. The whole construct of being gay was still pretty nebulous in those days. A gay friend of mine who I know from back then believes I was just oblivious, however. I think there is some truth to that.

I went from high school to college right away and it wasn't until then that things started changing for me. Some of my closer friends in college became involved with women, and I realized that I wasn't the least bit interested in anything sexual with women. That's when I started to pull back and look for something to read on the topic of homosexuality. The term *gay* was hardly used back then from what I recall. I was still not consciously acknowledging that I was gay, but I wondered what it all meant.

After two years of college, I went to West Africa to teach in a training college for two and a-half years. Those two years were among the most important in my life. I grew up a whole lot, and in most ways fairly positively. It really made me think about myself and the world that I lived in. People in this culture saw the world in different ways and did things in different ways. I started to refocus and think about who I was and what my values were.

My sense of religion evaporated quickly with that experience. My siblings and I all went to a Catholic grade school and church. I certainly had that ideology with all of its prescriptions about sex. I was surprised at how fast I just threw all that out. Distancing myself from my close-knit family helped.

I was sent to a place with two other fellows. After two weeks, one of them gave up on the whole thing and did absolutely the minimal amount of instruction. The second one eventually moved in that direction. I had a wonderful time, however. I was busy from the time I got there and learned a huge amount. I grew like mad. It was a great experience.

In the areas where I lived in West Africa, there were not the same kinds of moral prescriptions against sex, and it wasn't seen from a religious perspective. There was a great deal of spirituality, however, and sexuality had nothing to do with it. Sex play amongst younger kids was much more open and much more common. Even sexual intercourse was considerably more open. Families lived in small spaces and sexual activities between the mother and father took place with children present, maybe asleep or half asleep. It was not a big deal or this mysterious thing hidden away in the dark of night.

In two of the areas I lived, the father was not significant in child rearing. The mother's older brother was the one involved in raising the children with the mother's aid. The father was there primarily for sexual purposes. He had children that he supported from his sister. This sacred idea of the nuclear family raising their kids was thrown out the window for me. There was not a great deal of homosexuality that I was aware of or found, but there wasn't much prohibition about it either. Although there were prohibitions around some kinds of sexual activities (e.g., incest), in general there were fewer, and they were different from what I was used to.

My sojourn to Africa provided me with an opportunity to think about how we put our lives together and what things mean and why we give values to certain things. I wondered if some things I value in this society made any sense.

I ignored my sexuality while I was there. I was still looking at men but I was not doing much about it. Men in this society were significantly more affectionate with other men. Men commonly held hands when they walked together, and they often hugged one another. In the places I lived, men formed stronger bonds with men than with women.

I'll never forget one of the first days that I was there. A fellow talking to me just grabbed my hand as we walked. I nearly froze and fell over, I was so terrified. Then I realized that this was a common activity and I soon became comfortable with it. It probably meant more to me than the locals, however, as I started to fantasize about doing more than just holding hands and hugging, although it never went any further.

My gay awareness really began to explode when I left West Africa and returned to school. In total, I changed majors about eight times and attended six different universities. I completed a bachelor's degree in history and eventually returned and took a master's degree in early childhood education. Later, I returned and completed a second master's in special education with a major in early childhood.

The first few months back were difficult for me, probably one of the most difficult periods in my life. I had become so accustomed to another culture and society with differing values and beliefs. I was judging American society by the society I had been in. Many things seemed superficial.

When I returned, I became roommates with Joe, the gay friend I told you about earlier. While I was gone, he came to accept his gayness and was involved with some sexual activity with men, but he was still in the closet and hid this from me. As was typical at the time, we didn't talk about such things. I started to figure out what was happening, however, as I ran into a couple of men that he had been with sexually.

I then went off to another school and ended up in a city where I didn't know anyone. I shared an apartment with a fellow who had a couple of gay friends who were fairly obvious about it. These were the first people I knew who were visibly gay. I began meeting gay people who did not fit the stereotypes, and this really jarred me. One night I walked home from the library, and a guy pulled up in his car. He asked me for directions to get somewhere, but it was soon obvious that there was something else on his mind. He talked his way into coming back to my place and we had sex together.

It was a horrible experience, when I reflect on it. He was creepy, and I felt like I did something bad and dirty. I didn't have a strong sense of guilt, however, as my parents did not bring us up that way. I wondered, though, if that was what gay life was like. It bothered me a lot.

Shortly after that, I stopped at a friend's one evening. While walking back to my place, a fellow walked by and did the double look sort of thing. He ended up back at my place, and this turned out to be a totally different experience. It was wonderful. He soon figured out that I was pretty inexperienced and didn't know a lot about being gay. He was a few years older than me and was much more knowledgable. On a sexual level, this experience really changed things for me. I became sexually active from that time on with men and actively pursued it, but I still didn't admit that I was homosexual or gay. Instead, I ignored it.

Fréderic, 38

I lived in Quebec City for my first seventeen years of life. I have six older brothers, and two of them are also gay.

I was aware of some homoerotic interest from age ten through fourteen. My closest friends were good-looking boys, and although I wouldn't say I had major sexual fantasies for them, I clearly felt some erotic interest toward them. I was also attracted to certain actors in movies and on television. When I went swimming, I remember watching men in their trunks and in the showers: that was definitely the place to be. I knew that my clothed friends looked better without clothes. I also admit that some people I fantasized about at a young age were much older than me, which is still there. My dad used to sell magazines in his store, and I would buy gay magazines and use the pictures for fantasizing and masturbating.

My friends started dating girls from age thirteen, but I knew I was not similarly interested. I had sexual encounters with two women when I was fifteen or sixteen. It wasn't great, but it was good. I knew that it wasn't exactly what I wanted, though, because I found out that besides the bedroom, I wanted to experience an emotional connection to a male. I didn't want to learn about the straight world, because I wasn't attracted to that. At age seventeen, roughly, I became aware that I was attracted to men.

I did not interpret my emerging homoerotic feelings as negative. My parents did not have a positive attitude about gay people, however. According to my mother, they didn't know homosexuality existed. Their attitude slowed my coming out. Although I have two gay brothers, they had both left home by the time my homoerotic feelings fully surfaced. I was the last teen to be with my parents.

I think sexual orientation becomes more alive during the teenage years, and family is a powerful influence on its expression. I learned about my two brothers being gay in my late teen years. Although they acted as role models, I believe their effect was negative.

If you don't experience gayness with somebody outside the family situation, you don't really define it clearly for yourself. I needed to define my own gayness because I am somebody who believes strongly in my own independence and in my own self-determination. Although I had gay brothers around me, I decided that I would find out things for myself.

In high school I was involved in the school newspaper and I played sports. I was never confronted with the idea of being gay until one day another student told me that I was a faggot. That was the only time that I heard that, and it wasn't positive. I grew up in an environment where the word faggot was used in French more than the word gay.

My eldest gay brother and I shared the same bed when he came home for summers or holidays. From ages thirteen to fifteen, he had sex with me occasionally, which involved touch, masturbation, and oral sex. Clearly this was sexual abuse. He manipulated me by telling me that this was sex education, so I became his pupil. One of my straight brothers almost got it too. The abuse eventually stopped because I wasn't as nice as I used to be, and my eldest brother realized that I wasn't easy prey anymore.

My other gay brother knew about the incest, but he didn't tell anyone about it. When I came out about the incest two years ago, another brother asked me why I didn't tell anyone at the time. In my sexually repressed household, there was no way I could have done that.

Perhaps my brother woke up my sexual gayness. Unfortunately, this had two negative effects on me. First, it created impotence, which lasted for ten years. Second, it forced me to enter the world of gayness through incest. I'm still trying to resolve that.

Tommy, 41

I grew up in a small town in Nova Scotia. At its peak, the population was two thousand residents, and there were only twenty-two of us in my high school graduation class. Positive images of gay people didn't exist there. There was always talk about the school board secretary who sucked boys off. That was a common mythology when I was in high school, and it was considered horrible.

I wanted to leave this town from a young age, as there was nothing that stimulated me. There was no place to go to get experience. The focus was sports, and I wasn't good at them and I never really enjoyed them, either. No one wanted me on their team. I wanted to take music lessons, but my family didn't have the necessary resources.

I didn't have any real friends in high school, so I was quite isolated. I think I isolated myself. I remember that horrid feeling of trying to deny the fact that I was gay to avoid criticism.

I had been feeling sexually gay since I was really young. Some of the games I played as a preschooler contained sexual overtones. We used to take turns running around and pulling our pants down, and I found that highly erotic. As a youngster, I used to play this game with a peer in his father's workshop. I wanted to see his naked body.

I was called a faggot more than most kids. My brother, for

example, played hockey, so he fit in better. My brother had many friends, but I didn't. I was just different enough. Because my mother was a teacher, kids didn't like her. I think they took out their frustrations toward her on me. I remember getting beat up on the way to school and back from school.

I definitely had sexual fantasies at age ten. There was a kid in my class that I daydreamed about, wanting to be with him naked and see him naked. I remember sneaking peaks at muscle magazines and actually stealing pornographic magazines when I was around ten years old. I remember getting a brochure in the mail once that had a picture of the statue of David in his glorious nudeness. I kept that under my pillow for months. These unclad pictures became important parts of my sexual fantasies.

I was conscious in grade seven that I didn't particularly like women. I finally had a date with a girl, and I felt embarrassed about going to a dance with her. I thought she was really nice, but I wasn't motivated. It didn't make sense to me. It was around this time that I started distinguishing between guys I found attractive and those I didn't.

I tried asking girls out on dates in high school, but I didn't feel like I fit into the straight community. My self-image remained really low. There was a particular guy in my class that I found stimulating, and we used to sit next to each other for a couple of classes. I felt a strong attraction toward him.

Wanting to learn about homosexuality, I turned to books like the *Encyclopedia Britannica* and the *World Book of Knowledge*, but they did not provide particularly positive images or ideas about it. I was finding male bodies very stimulating, but I couldn't legitimately accept these feelings. I didn't feel good about having homoerotic attractions as a teenager. That was a really negative period for me. By the time I was out of high school, I really didn't like myself and I didn't have any friends. I was insecure for a long period in my life.

I had my first sexual experience with a male when I was eighteen. My forty-year-old cousin-in-law, Jerry, seduced me. Although he was married with two kids, I suspect that seducing young boys was something he did periodically. I knew the whole score. I think I had fantasized this was going to happen before it actually happened. One night we camped out together and he got me drunk. Then he suggested that I sleep with him, and that's where it started. It went on for about a year. He was an alcoholic, which was a bad scene for me. It seemed that for many years I became attracted to alcoholic homosexuals. I believe this experience with my cousin-in-law was largely to blame.

After the affair with Jerry, I felt total denial of having experienced gay sexuality. I didn't have the self-confidence to believe that my feelings were legitimate. I wanted to be like everyone else. I thought having sexual relationships with women would help, and although it happened a few times, I didn't find it particularly satisfying.

I wasn't at that point classified as a faggot, but other kids in that community were, and it was viewed very negatively. I wanted to leave my hometown, so in 1976, I moved to a major city and attended university. This was definitely a quest to seek out gay people.

While reading sociology, I began to realize that stigma is something ascribed to you and not something you are. That helped me understand that being gay itself was not a negative thing. Realizing that society's values may conflict with your own helped me accept my own individuality—that being gay is legitimate and that I'm okay.

Cliff, 30

My life began in a small town west of Calgary. I've always known that I was gay and I think my mom knew too. Even as a young child, I felt like a normal kid with a secret. I knew I was different, but I didn't have a label for it.

My mother put me in figure skating at age five, and two years later I picked up hockey as well. I figure skated in the early morning, followed immediately by hockey. The other hockey players came onto the ice as I switched from my figure skates to my hockey skates. They used to razz me a lot, saying things like, "Well, you know, only girls figure skate." Nothing I found really hurtful.

Then once during a regular scrimmage game, I got struck near my eye with a hockey stick. It could have blinded me if it had been an inch closer. I decided that I was not going to play a game where people are actually trying to hurt me. If I was going to be on the ice, I would be the one to hurt myself by wiping out on figure skates. I subsequently quit hockey. I still like to play sports, but I am not big on watching them.

I was a nellie child, but I never put myself down for it. I've never felt that I was unworthy or bad. I remember being called a fag even before I knew what it meant, but everybody called everybody a fag in my school. The girls were bitches and the guys were fags.

At around age seven or eight, I remember checking out guys in the change room at the outdoor swimming pool and at the hockey arena. The junior hockey team was ages sixteen to twenty. I frequently went to watch these guys run around in their jock straps because I enjoyed it immensely. Although I noticed the guys with great bodies, that was about it. I didn't have actual sexual feelings toward males until somewhere between ages eleven and thirteen. I never thought it was wrong to look.

As for cross-gender behaviors—since I grew up to be a drag queen—my brother, sister, cousins and I would dress up in grandma's playroom when I was young. All of us dressed up as girls. There were no boy clothes there. I always used to wear this yellow dress.

I was just being a ham. I'm entertaining, and I like to put on a show. Some people think I'm on twenty-four hours a day and constantly thinking of something to say or do or be silly. I am when I'm at work, and sometimes when I'm at home. It's not so much that I need attention, but I just get on a roll and suddenly it's happening: the laughs and the fun. I just knew there was something there. When I was a kid, I didn't think of cross-dressing regularly or doing drag; that came years later. When I did, though, I thought, "Yep, I can do this."

Paul, 50

I was born in Airdrie, Alberta but lived in a small coal-mining town for my first year and a half of life. Then we moved to various towns in British Columbia. I remained in British Columbia until I moved back to Alberta in 1977.

I knew there was something different about me from the time I was five or six years old. I was sexually attracted to boys from age five, and I was not attracted to girls. There was one boy that I often fantasized about. I didn't really know anything about sex, but the emotional side of it was there. I also wanted to get physically close to him.

I was eleven when I had my first sexual experience, and it was wonderful. He was fifteen or sixteen, and we had oral sex and masturbated together. I continued to have sexual experiences with him and one other guy until I was sixteen or seventeen years old. I eventually closed the door on it because I internalized what society and people believed about it. I thought what I did was wrong. On the other hand, though, I wondered how my feelings toward males could be so wrong when they felt so right. It's really hard as a child to think that your feelings are wrong.

I believe that society's values really did a number on me. I was raised in the fifties and sixties, and being gay was considered unacceptable. It was something not talked about, period. If you were then gay or homosexual, you were thought of as a pervert: you were this, you were that, and you should be locked up. The view was also that if you really wanted to, you could change. That made it much harder for me to come to terms with my own self. I was smart enough to keep quiet for fear of being locked up in an institution. I knew I didn't belong there.

I would be called everything at school, but I don't think anyone knew I was gay. I was not a jock because of medical reasons, though I wanted to play baseball and other sports. That alienated me right there. The macho sports enthusiasts called anybody who was not in their realm a fag. According to them, a lot of kids must have been fags in those days!

I grew up with a great deal of hate and animosity toward my father. I haven't talked to him in twenty-seven years. He was always the type of person that insists you do as he tells you and you aren't allowed to question him. I have a different attitude about that, though. Nobody tells Paul what to do, and we didn't get along for that simple reason. He was an abusive man, physically, and he was six-foot-three and 225 pounds. By comparison, I was six feet and a lot lighter.

After moving away from home, I sought adventure. I wanted to see what else was out there and I did it. I accepted every opportunity to get transferred that came up in the company I worked for. I wanted new experiences and new challenges, and I went for it.

After age seventeen, I ceased having further sexual experiences with males until I was about twenty-four or twenty-five. At age twenty, I did what society expected: I got married and had kids. My ex-wife remains the only woman I was ever with sexually. I suppressed my feelings so much that I was determined to make my marriage work, come hell or high water.

The biggest mistake anybody can make is to get married if they are homosexual, however. Eventually your feelings surface, and they create more problems for you. Then you've got somebody else's life involved, and perhaps children as well. My same-sex feelings started emerging again, as I could no longer suppress them. My marriage and everything else started going downhill.

John, 61

I distinctly remember the first time my father took me on a holiday with him, when I was seven. We were on a train and we slept in the same berth. I remember feeling enthralled with becoming entwined in my father's legs. I think that is my first memory of being attracted to males. I don't think I paid any attention to his penis, but rather I just remember the feeling of being close to this nice male person who happened to be my father.

My father was a successful businessman and he was also a highly decorated soldier in two World Wars. My family was socially prominent in Edmonton, and my mother was very conscious of her position. Both of my parents thought it was important to be well connected. I could see some things that I just didn't like about that lifestyle. From observing guests at my parent's parties, I concluded that some people in our social strata were inauthentic. While one side of me wanted to be successful and prominent like my parents, the other side of me was developing an understanding of how phony some people were about their real feelings on subjects and their actual commitment to society. However, I never failed to respect my father for his deep sense of duty and loyalty to his country and, in those years, to the Crown.

During my early teenage years I became aware that I was not developing the same attitude toward the opposite sex as most of my friends, and I became very conscious of my attraction to males. I dealt with that in general by suppressing it and leading a straight and conventional lifestyle. At that time I was at one of Canada's most established boarding schools for boys. I participated in many sports and school activities and became a leader in the school. That also kept me on the straight and narrow.

Nonetheless, I did have some sexual encounters during those teenage years, which I found pleasurable. I can remember feeling huge pangs of guilt in high school soon after having an orgasm with another guy.

I first fell in love with a heterosexual friend of mine when I was in grade ten. I did everything possible to be with him: I did everything he did and liked everything he liked. That lasted throughout high school and beyond. I didn't then understand why I had these feelings. I tried to suppress them, but they continued for many years.

I went on to university and joined a fraternity. It became apparent to me that one young alumnus in the fraternity paid a lot of attention to me. At first I found it flattering and I enjoyed this person's company. However, at the end of my second year of university, I went on a trip with him to the United States, and something turned me off about him. He came on to me in a way that left me feeling that I couldn't handle it. I decided then and there that I did not want to continue any physical relationship with him. I clearly remember that I vowed I was going to do my best to shut down those feelings, and I did. It was at least ten years later when I started feeling that I was really being deprived or depriving myself of my whole being…my real sexuality.

I think mostly what kept me in the closet was that I wanted to become a productive, successful member of society. I wanted to finish my law degree and practice in an established firm in Edmonton. It was also because of social standing.

I decided I would get married. I met a girl at university from a similar background to myself a few months after my American trip. I had known of her before. We had attended the same Protestant church, and her father was a well-known professional in Edmonton. I certainly enjoyed her company and thought that she was really nice and a lot of fun. I ceased to have any sexual connection with any other male. We had a happy marriage in the earlier years, but on the sexual side, I realized I was not fulfilled at all. I was going through an exercise whenever my wife and I had sex. It was almost meaningless for me.

As I entered my late thirties, I began to feel that I was missing something that everybody else was enjoying. I began to really question whether I should remain married. Those feelings became stronger, which I think were exacerbated by the fact that gay people were starting to be accepted and talked about in a positive way. In the late 1970s, there was definitely a growing acceptance of gay people, especially amongst the more educated. Ten or fifteen years before that, the subject was simply not discussed.

I was not in love with my wife the way I subsequently fell in love with a male. That happened to me about fifteen years after we were married. I met the person by accident, and I fell totally in love with him. Having that to compare to, I realized I was never in love with my wife to that degree. When I fell in love with that man, I didn't ever want to be away from him.

He was respectful of the fact that I was married and had children, so it wasn't that I saw him three times a week or anything like that. We went hiking together, sometimes accompanied by my son. My wife got to know him a little, and I think she liked him. This relationship was the catalyst that helped me to come out to myself. I let myself be really what I am. Unfortunately, he died in a canoe accident about two years after I met him. This totally devastated me. My wife even came to the funeral with me, and she was actually very supportive. She was also not aware that we were having a relationship at that time, but she later put it together.

Although I developed a feeling that I could cope on my own, I didn't really know what to expect in my law firm. I was then a partner in a conservative and established practice in Edmonton. By this time, my wife had become suspicious that I was gay, so she had gone independently and secretly for counseling and finally persuaded me to come with her.

The psychiatrist told my wife that he thought I was dedicated to her and that I actually loved her but that if she wanted the marriage to survive, she would have to recognize that I would need to have a more open relationship. She rejected that. It became clear that we wouldn't reconcile our differences.

We separated around six months later. I literally walked out of the house on a summer day in the late 1970s. The children were then ages eleven, fourteen, and sixteen: Kathy, Gordon, and Susan, respectively. I was forty-two years old. We had stayed married for eighteen years.

David, 16

My parents have been divorced since I was three years old. I used to see my father every Sunday until about four years ago. I never enjoyed these visits. He wouldn't do a lot with me, and when he did, it felt obligatory. Consequently, I never became close to him. I haven't had any contact with him since I was twelve.

A couple of years before that, I confronted my father and said, "You aren't being a really good dad to me." He responded with, "Well, okay, if you want to see me, you call me." For the first while I called him, but whenever I did, he was always busy. He made no effort to see me, so I finally quit trying. He already had. That has affected me in a big way. It hurts when I see other families with a mother and father.

I have had cerebral palsy since I was a baby. That is why my fine motor skills are impaired. Besides cerebral palsy, I also have obsessive-compulsive disorder. I sometimes check the lock on the door repetitively, and I worry excessively about my health and other things that have no foundation. I have been home from school recently for two weeks because of my anxiety.

When I was around four years old, I remember asking my mother, "Do men ever marry?" She replied, "They do if things are right for them." That was probably my first inkling of being gay. As I grew older, I thought about it more.

Around age six, I used to go to the swimming pool with my father. I remember being very attracted to men in the change rooms. That also gave me the idea that maybe I'm different. My dad would always say, "Whatcha looking at?" I couldn't answer because I was so embarrassed.

One memory from when I was about eight really sticks out in my mind. I had a friend that I really liked, and we spent considerable time together. I actually told him that I loved him, and he responded back to me similarly. Later I found out that he was the school bully. He apparently wasn't nice to most of our peers, but he was to me. I feel that was the beginning for me of my gay awareness.

I thought about it for the next few years, but I didn't really want to say anything about it. I was afraid of it. I'm already physically challenged, and I thought I didn't need the extra complication of being gay. I thought gay is just another thing on top of that and I'm not going to be gay.

I kept refusing to think about it until I was around thirteen. I decided to approach my school counselor, and I told her that I thought I was gay. She gave me some information on a youth group in Calgary, and I went to the center once and met some people. I became really uncomfortable with it after that and decided not to go back for a year and a half.

Glenn, 46

I was not aware that I was different in my childhood years. I played with boys and girls equally. I know I felt an attraction toward females in my mid-to-late teens, which continued until my mid-twenties. To my recollection, I was not conscious then of being attracted to males. When I was in that age bracket, I didn't like the way I looked, so when I did notice another guy, I thought about having his hair, clothes, face, or body. There was really nothing overtly sexual about it.

My family moved when I was fifteen, and I found myself in a high school where I knew nobody. That changed after I became involved with a large circle of friends from the church youth group. My social life was active with this group throughout high school and university. We did everything together. If any of us were sexually active, we never talked about it. I suspect that by and large we were not.

Growing up in Calgary, I didn't realize that there were options available. I did not know there was such a thing as homosexuality. Call it naiveté. I was slow in developing sexual interest and awareness. I never even masturbated seriously until I was twenty or twenty-one, and I do not remember entertaining sexual fantasies. I was simply pleasing myself. Sexual matters were hush-hush throughout society, and sex was something that was never discussed at either home or school.

I began attending the University of Alberta in 1967 to pursue a bachelor of arts in romance languages. In my own way, I'm a quiet rebel and by the time the seventies rolled around, drugs and free love were everywhere. I basically said, "Well, that's really not for me." I made my own choices, and that was not a scene I wanted. Sex was not a big deal to me either. I suppose I could take it or leave it, and I think I was stuck in that mode where you saved yourself for somebody special whom you would eventually marry.

Soon after graduating, I moved back to Calgary and began

working. In the mid-seventies, at the age of twenty-six, I traveled to England. English men generally paid more attention to their grooming and their dress than Albertans. For the first time, I really started looking at men. Something clicked inside me that I could be exactly who I wanted to be and what I wanted to be in England. With money to burn, I could do just about anything I wanted. It was a liberating experience for me. There were none of the restraints and restrictions that I faced at home.

Nonetheless, I never really thought much about it at the time. I know that I felt good about myself when I returned home. My body image problem was resolved and I really liked myself. I wasn't really aware of any big change, but my friends and family were. My sister had asked my mother: "What's happened to Glenn? He's a whole new person!"

Visiting England became an annual event. My third trip was in 1978, and this is when I became aware of having homosexual inclinations. I stayed with Brian, a heterosexual friend of mine from Edmonton who was doing his Ph.D. in London. He enjoyed walking at night; it was his thinking time. One night we went out for a walk through Holland Park. I was surprised by all of the men there at one or two in the morning. Years later I discovered that it was then one of London's most popular and notorious outdoor cruising areas.

Brian kidded with me by saying, "Don't worry, they're all fags." I chuckled, but—call it what you will—an animal instinct began stirring within me. Although I found this frightening, I was drawn toward it. I wondered if maybe I belonged there, in Holland Park, at night. A seed was germinating, because I was still relatively ignorant about homosexuality.

Following this night, I did a lot of thinking about it. I visited some dirty book shops and looked over magazines of men. The dirty book scene in England has magazines for every taste: heterosexual, homosexual, you name it. Every kink. Some of it is really far out and bizarre. I found it very exciting. That was the first time that I had ever found publications like that, because Calgary and Edmonton were still in the backwoods.

I took the night ferry to France a few days later. I sat alone in a compartment until two men joined me. The younger one, an American, told me that he was an actor and then said, "You don't mind if I change my shirt, do you? I've been in this all day." He took great pains to change his shirt very, very slowly in front of me. I'm sure I was supposed to take notice of his exhibitionistic parade. I did, but it didn't do anything for me. I suspect this guy was gay and he had an eye for me.

Nonetheless, I put these developing interests on the back burner and returned to Calgary in mid July. In August, I began frequenting a park that was known as a place where men gathered. Whether or not there was sex going on, I don't know. I would often go down to that park and sunbathe to get a glimpse. I was curious, but nothing happened.

In 1979, I was again in France. I walked along the bank of the Seine in Paris one sunny afternoon and found a bunch of men sunbathing, clad only in undershorts, lying on towels. I joined them. I never thought anything of it, and only recently did I discover that this area, near the Orangerie, is one of Paris' biggest cruising areas and has been since the sixteenth or seventeenth century.

In Calgary in the spring of 1980, I met a young woman, Sharon. She was gorgeous, with beautiful hair and eyes, a lovely figure, and an exceptional personality. Although I was extremely attracted to her, I was unable to take the relationship beyond the level of a very good friendship. I didn't understand why.

Toward the end of the summer, she moved to Ontario and reconnected with an old boyfriend. They became engaged, and I was devastated. I went off to England a few weeks later, and it started gelling in my mind that something was not right. I was angry, actually, that I had let this wonderful woman get away from me. I was also angry that I had remained celibate for so many years. I kept thinking that this was really a crock of shit. I decided it was time to reexamine my outlook on life and my philosophy toward sex and marriage.

I soon decided to start getting my fair share of sex, and I didn't really care whether it would be with men or women. That's when I started to deal with the gay issue. During my next trip to England, I went to a gay bar for the first time. A great surge of attraction to men was exploding concurrently with an attraction to fetishes and leather sex. These issues were starting to bubble around in an overwhelming pot.

In 1981, I actually picked somebody up in a local park one day. I had been cruising him for weeks and I went back to his apartment. We didn't have sex, but I really enjoyed the physical closeness, the touching, and the affection. It scared me as I was still walking the tightrope about which way I was going to fall, and it eventually got shoved to the background because I wasn't ready. Things happen when they're ready to happen, and if we sum up my life story, that's exactly what occurred. Things happened for me when the time was right.

I found 1982 through 1984 to be the most difficult time of my life. I experienced a lot of inward thinking and soul searching. I was trying to come to grips with my sexual orientation and the way that I wanted to express myself sexually. I think what I really needed then was human companionship with others who had similar sexual interests. Unfortunately, Calgary was still a backward city. I felt very lonely.

I was dealing with many stereotypes. For example, I believed homosexuality was something that you kept secret and only expressed after dark. It was something that wasn't really socially acceptable. It was especially difficult in our society then to develop a positive gay identity. Dealing with the leather aspect also made me wonder if I was a monster. I thought I would never find fulfilment because I thought I was the only one with similar interests. It was a sad, tragic, and difficult time for me.

Troy, 24

I'm from a small town near Ottawa of three thousand. Nobody was out in either junior or senior high school. Nobody ever asked me if I was gay because I didn't have any of the stereotypical traits. People had no reason to suspect.

But I have felt different since I was three years old. I remember sitting on my uncle's lap at around age six and thinking that it was really exciting compared to sitting on my aunt's or my mom's lap. I don't believe you can really have a sexual attraction or urge as a young child, but there was something there.

Even before the age of five, I had dolls and I played dress up. I remember a couple of times finding my mom's makeup and letting loose with it. My dad built me a play house. None of my male friends had them but my female friends had something similar. I don't remember negative reactions from anybody. My interests were actually quite varied. I also went to the pond and caught frogs.

I remember being on a trip with my parents when I was twelve. I had a sexual dream of being with another guy. For the rest of the trip I couldn't get this off my mind. Thinking about the experience in the dream felt really exciting and good, so why did I feel so bad about myself? The dream made me realize the way in which I was different, and another part of me thought, "I cannot accept this." This began my battle against it.

I don't have any memories of attraction before adolescence. During my adolescence I thought a lot about sex…with guys. I always remember thinking, "This is just a phase. Next year I'll outgrow this." It never happened.

I was starting to look a lot at men. I remember being attracted to classmates and to gym teachers. When I masturbated, all of my sexual fantasies involved men. I tried to fantasize about women, but it wasn't there. I felt guilty about my homosexual fantasies.

I first had a sexual experience when I was in grade thirteen. I was at a party, and I drank a lot of alcohol. A woman blew me. Although I felt no attraction toward her, I remember thinking that maybe there was hope for me yet.

I became more sexual when I was attending the University of Waterloo, when I was nineteen. I developed a relationship that fall with a woman named Jodine. We had a great relationship, including sexually. She had an aggressive personality, and I think that is what enabled us to develop a sexual relationship—she initiated it and I went along for the ride. If it had been left up to me, it probably would never have happened. During sex, I continued to fantasize about men.

I thought I was on top of the world because I finally had what was socially acceptable. We were together for two years, but I continued thinking about guys. As the relationship became more serious, I became frightened. We started having trouble getting along and neither of us remained happy. She eventually ended the relationship.

I know that I hung on toward the end because our relationship was like a security blanket. I had what society and my family expected of me. We saw each other off and on through that, but it was hard. I was pretty depressed for the first half of 1994.

Toward the spring, there was a girl who was attracted to me. We were in classes together and went out a few times. I ended up back at her place, and she wanted things to happen, but there was nothing. I just wanted to get out of there fast. Afterwards I felt so embarrassed and stupid. What was I doing? This wasn't what I wanted. I knew the direction I was about to take. I had to explore the other side.

Andrew, 29

In many ways, I think we create our story and once set, I'm not sure how much we revisit it. For the past five years, my perspective has been that it was easy. When I think about it today, however, I think it was actually quite hard.

It was a long process for me. Like many gay people, I had the perception that I was different, but I didn't know that I was queer. As a young teenager, my awareness began to change because of my sister's experience.

Karen moved out on her sixteenth birthday and moved in with an older man. On her eighteenth birthday, she married him. The marriage lasted less than a year, and after that she traveled through Europe. When she returned, she told my two brothers and me that she was a lesbian. Then she came out to our parents, and that was when I really started thinking about my own sexuality.

There were many really negative consequences in our home around her disclosure. My parents were pretty horrible about how they dealt with her, and they ended up completely isolating her from the house. She tried to be part of my life by coming to school and hanging out with me, but Mom and Dad didn't know about it.

Her experience reinforced for me that coming out was a bad and dangerous thing to do. It cost her a lot in terms of her relationship with Dad and her ability to have a relationship with us. Although her disclosure may have sped up my questioning of my own gayness, it may have delayed my eventual decision to live as an out gay man. Either way, her coming out is very much wrapped up in my process.

My dad's father was a police officer, and he was very negative about homosexuality in his working years. That message got conveyed to Dad. My mother grew up in a much more liberal, well-educated family of doctors. It took five to seven years of strained relationships before my parents could deal with Karen's sexuality. They were blatantly homophobic. Karen's also political and in-your-face, which added an extra layer of challenge for my parents.

With Karen's influence, I got a much better political grasp on being gay than most children would receive. I quickly realized that I was gay and what it meant. I had sexual fantasies about males, not females, and I knew I was really attracted to guys. I knew what the power issues were and what it meant for me and how it could or would affect my life. Even as I saw progress with Mom and Dad and Karen, I knew it would be different for me because I was male. I started dealing with it quietly.

When I was sixteen or seventeen, my parents were afraid that maybe I was also gay, and they asked me. I completely denied it. I was afraid to disclose to them because earlier they had threatened Karen that if I or one of my brothers turned out gay, they would never forgive her.

I didn't want to be gay in high school, so I stayed busy with other stuff. I had girlfriends and I enjoyed some sexual activity with them. I wanted to have a place in the straight world. I hoped I would change and become heterosexual, but I knew I wouldn't.

I attended a liberal and accepting high school. There was one guy there that everyone knew was gay. He was incredibly flaming. He was so totally outrageous that everyone loved him because they didn't know what else to make of him. He could get away with being who he was. Although I was totally aware of gay identity, I knew that I couldn't have it yet. This wasn't the time or the place.

I nearly had a sexual experience with a guy when I was in grade eleven. We spent a lot of time together over a couple of weeks. He really wanted something to happen and he constantly pushed me, but I wasn't ready. I slept over one night and we talked about masturbation. I ended up watching him masturbate, and then we talked about it. I was petrified to go near him or touch him for fear that someone would catch us.

In grade thirteen, I had my first sexual experience with a guy. I knew it was going to happen, so I let it happen. After that experience, I acted like a total prick and disappeared completely out of his life. I didn't talk to him again or return his phone calls. I was a pig in thinking that he was "too gay" for me. I still regret how I ended it with him. Nonetheless, it was a confirming experience. I felt that I did what I needed to do, but then I put it away and decided I would have to deal with it later. That would only happen when I was no longer in this town and away from Mom and Dad.

After attending Carleton University briefly, I relocated and studied liberal arts at McGill. My prime motive for moving away to university was not to discover my sexuality; I wanted to have different life experiences, see the rest of the country, and meet new and interesting people. I wanted to escape my banal existence in Ontario. I knew about my sexuality, and I wasn't ready to deal with it. The rest of my life was more important.

I worked in the Columbia ice fields during the summers. Between forty and fifty of us worked together, and we got to know each other really well. I developed some incredible crushes on people there. We lived in a maze of Atco trailers, and I slept with different people in a completely nonsexual way. It was a trusting, open environment.

Alex, 23

I was born outside Ottawa on a native reserve. Within three months, I was apprehended by the Children's Aid Society and went into foster care, where I spent just under the first year-and-a-half of my life.

I was adopted by a white family, and we moved around Ontario. My native ancestry was never discussed. In the last four or five years, I've really begun learning about my nation and first-nation issues in general. I am gradually identifying with my native heritage. By law, I can classify for native-treaty status once I find family-of-origin information about my birth mother. I've placed my name on the register in Ontario to try to connect with her. It's a long process.

As far as I know, my birth father was from Ireland. It was a short-lived relationship between him and my mother—probably about forty-five minutes. To my knowledge, he had no idea that I ever existed.

At age six, I knew I was different from my family in the sense of skin color and hair color. Until I reached puberty, I was very dark-skinned. As I've gotten older, I've become whiter. No one ever assumes I am native.

I was also different in another sense. I remember having crushes on boys as early as grade one, and I also knew this was wrong. I lived in a small town, and gay people were described as sick individuals. I chased girls so I would fit in.

Growing up with my adoptive parents was not a positive event in my life. I officially lived with them until I was fifteen, but until I was twelve, I watched my father physically and emotionally abuse my mother. He was a very angry man and a poor communicator of both thoughts and feelings. He was a high-ranking RCMP officer who gradually became an alcoholic. My parents are relatively well-off, and we always lived in a nice house. We learned to keep our family secrets to ourselves. I remember Dad getting Mom on the floor and striking her. At age six or seven, I would try to stop it. After her assault would end, she would start on me. I was abused physically and emotionally. Both of them would continually put me down, calling me a liar, cheat, thief, and a momma's boy.

In retrospect, I suppose I earned many of their adjectives. I stole, I lied, and I fought. I lied to teachers about trivial things so I would get caught. I remember sitting in the principal's office, crying and begging, "Please don't call my parents, please don't, I can't go home. Can I stay at the school?"

The principal wouldn't listen. He always phoned my mother, and after I got home, she would tell me to wait until Dad arrived. Once home, he would remove his belt and say, "So what have you done today?" That was the worst experience.

When I turned twelve, it all started changing. I was maturing physically, and I became more of a target for physical abuse. Whenever I tried to help Mother during her assaults, Dad would hit me and send me to my room. He would strike me in the face, throw me on the floor, or push and shove me.

I struggled in school, not from a lack of brains, but because I wanted to struggle. I wanted somebody to say, "Hey, why are you failing gym in grade five?" My brother, who is their natural child, received preferential treatment. He rarely experienced my father's abuse. He moved at age fifteen to attend university. He had skipped grades three and five and finished high school in Ontario in three years, instead of the customary five. He was happy that he didn't have to live at home anymore.

At age six, I was sexually abused by a twenty-year-old cousin. That summer we were in New Brunswick and I slept in a tent with him. Although my memories are vague, there was touching involved, and I performed oral sex on him. One of the hardest things for me to struggle with as a teenager was whether or not I liked it. The sexual behaviour was exciting and daring, and I thought my cousin must really like me to show me his penis. I thought it was all right.

Like many male victims of sexual abuse, I didn't see it as abuse. I didn't make the connection that this person was twenty and I was six. I have often thought about this abuse. I was angry with myself because by the time I was eight or nine, everyone on the school yard knew what faggots were, so I assumed I was a faggot.

Around the age of eight or nine, I started hanging out with three other boys my age and we would show and touch each other's genitals. I think we even tried to penetrate each other. We did this in different places, often at someone's house during a sleepover. No one saw this as a bad thing. It continued until we were probably thirteen or so.

One Saturday afternoon when I was twelve years old, I was at the games arcade when a guy offered me a cigarette. I took it because I wanted to be cool. Then he offered me a ride home, and while we drove away, he said, "Do you mind if we stop at my place?" I replied, "Not at all." Once there, he asked me if I did drugs, and I said, "Yes." In truth, I had never done drugs in my life. Then he began playing a gay porn movie.

My head raced as I thought, "This is bad, this is bad. Alex, you're being bad. Your parents will kill you." I knew he wanted sex. As he started touching my leg, I became uncomfortable. He said, "I can give you drugs for it if you want." That became my introduction to drugs. I smoked a cocaine joint and thought, "Wow, this feels great." I sat in his apartment all afternoon. We did drugs, he touched me, I sucked him off, and that was it. He was around thirty years old.

I went home and threw up. I was sick with myself that I had seen the porn movies, and I knew that I had just done something wrong. Nonetheless—I have no idea why—I had given him my phone number.

I remember the day he phoned. I met him at my street corner and we went back to his apartment again, but this time he had a friend visiting. Throughout the night I did lines of cocaine for the first time, and I had sex with both of them. His friend gave me thirty dollars, which was like half a week's paper delivery.

I thought he liked me, but let's be honest—he didn't like me. He gave me attention, bought me lunch, told me how smart and how nice I was, and complemented me on my looks. Our sexual liaisons continued.

One day we were at McDonald's, and he began talking to a teenager. I was getting pissed off, wondering what the fuck was going on. I felt incredibly jealous. The teen finally left, but we drove by him later that night. We picked him up and took him by the river. He was waiting for someone to pick him up. That was when I learned about prostitution.

One night I walked down to the river by myself. I was curious. Although I told myself that I wouldn't do it with anybody, that soon changed. By the end of the night a guy had given me twenty dollars for sucking him off. He was over fifty.

He gave me the attention I wanted. I'm sure I would have done it for free at that point. I knew I couldn't explain the money to my parents, so I ate twenty dollars worth of McDonald's food before going home.

I continued seeing the thirty-year-old. The cocaine became the reason I would see him—not the sex, the money, or the attention. I think I used cocaine partly to avoid the realization that I was gay. In my mind, I was there for the drugs—not the sex. I believed that what I was doing was wrong. I knew that if my friends found out that I was having sex with this guy, they would all freak, and they'd beat me up because faggots were not good. Nonetheless, I was still getting it on with the friends I mentioned earlier who were my age.

I also started sleeping with girls when I was twelve. I honestly grew up thinking everybody was getting it on. All my friends were. We would go to parties when we were twelve and thirteen, and there was definitely a lot of sex happening. They were all smoking dope and drinking too.

By age thirteen, I knew I liked the sexual activity and that it made me feel good. I started thinking I might be gay. Things at home were just horrible and by now I knew all of the bad downtown kids. One of them, a sixteen-year-old named George, was going to Vancouver, and I went with him. I cleaned out my bank account and ran away.

An older friend of George's arranged a hotel room for us in Vancouver. I began prostituting. I became familiar with the gay ghetto in Vancouver and hung out with hustlers and prostitutes. After five or six weeks, I returned home.

I also returned to school. I was clean, I got a haircut, and I started selling drugs. I was now a cocaine addict. I went to this party where they were all smoking dope and I said "Hey man, I've got something that's way cooler than that." I pulled out some cocaine and no one in this room had ever seen it. People started loving it. Within five months, several senior students at my school were using cocaine on a weekly basis. A year later, many of them had become daily users. I blame a great deal of that on myself.

I got hooked up with boys in New York who started supplying the school with drugs. Once drugs became involved, violence erupted. The school didn't know what to do. I was on student council, and pretty well everyone on council was coked out except one Mormon girl.

Everyone liked me at school, and I was a good fighter. No one could take me down. If someone needed someone beat up, I would do it. I just didn't have a conscience. I wouldn't need a reason to beat someone up, either. If someone looked at me funny in class, I would freak out on them.

By the time I was fifteen, I had used every drug that was available on the street. Eventually a large drug bust occurred at my school, and although I was connected to everybody, I wasn't charged or even arrested. In response, my parents sent me to Toronto to live with my aunt and uncle.

The friend who had brought me to Vancouver a year earlier was beaten to death. I remember that day because I thought I was a tough guy, I'm strong, I'm rich, and it doesn't matter to me. However, I started asking myself, "What am I involved in? Where am I? What am I doing?" I decided that I needed to get clean.

The first night at my relatives', I went to the mall and I smoked a joint with these other kids. I remember telling myself, "No, I can't do that." The worst thing I did after that was smoke cigarettes.

It went really well for about six months. School was going better than ever, mostly because I had no friends, and I didn't know anyone. I didn't have anything else to do. Then I began thinking more about being gay. I would meet people and hint that I was gay.

Chapter Four
Before Coming Out Summary of Themes

The Experience of Gay Men

Before coming out, we suffer varying degrees of psychological conflict. The war inside can feel like mortal combat. It is our humanness that is at stake. So many things inform us that we are different (i.e., the *catalysts*), yet so many things block our awareness and acceptance (i.e., the *hindrances*).

The catalysts pry our eyes open. A developing awareness of being gay and gay culture emerges while our sexual orientation manifests itself. When our vision is clear, we are very aware that we feel different from heterosexual men. Our sexual fantasies and dreams draw our attention to homoeroticism. Our arousal and attraction toward men is strong, and if we have the inner strength and opportunity during this early period, some of us experience homosexual acts. Even without this chance, however, we are informed by our feelings. Falling in love and feeling pangs of infatuation give us away in our hearts. Many of us had sexual experiences with women, but something was lacking. Either our enjoyment was compromised, or our ability to fall deeply in love was thwarted. Few of us understood why, early on. That took some soul-searching and further life experience.

Some of us broached our sexuality from a different angle. The excitement caused by a fetish or a desire to entertain could evoke an interest in leather and/or female drag. If the interest was persistent enough, it would later become integrated into identity.

Eventually, all of us had to begin an inside journey. The questioning and soul searching begged for an answer we could accept. At some level we usually knew what had to be faced, but our hope, like that of our families, was that it would pass. As the inside journey continued, we began our tentative steps outward. Exploring the gay world took us in different directions, and we began wherever it felt safe. Some of us moved to different residences before taking the next step. Some turned to others to help them face what they knew to be true.

While our eyes were being opened, other forces tried to close them again, sometimes so successfully in fact that they stayed closed for many years. The hindrances boil down to one thing: the fear and condemnation of homosexuals, both internally and externally. This demon is named *homophobia*, and it has a life of its own. Beginning at the societal level, it infiltrates the minds of citizens, who inadvertently, if not deliberately, keep it alive and well. The stereotypes degrade us, and the victimization we suffer is cloaked in a veil of silence. Many don't know we exist, but the demon knows, and it comes out whenever the terrible silence is broken. Some scramble to make sense of something that makes no sense to them. Others continue to deny that homosexuality exists. Still others lash out verbally or physically, trying to rid the earth symbolically of the demon. The demon they're fighting lies within.

Unfortunately, very unfortunately, the demon has even entered the minds of those who are trying to come out. Nearly all of us have fought to overcome *internalized homophobia*, which is our own fear and hatred of ourselves. Raised to believe that we are sinners, we have religious and societal guilt buried deep in our psyches. The desire to run is strong, and many do. While the frantic running continues, our self-esteem suffers. We try hard to minimize our feelings, and sometimes we are so good at it that we deny who we are for years or decades. Our presentation to others is that we are heterosexuals, and some of us manage to hold back our feelings by focusing our energies on other things. During this charade, it's not uncommon that we become extremely productive and work ourselves into the ground. After all, we don't love ourselves all that much. A symbolic death is perhaps the best we can muster.

Some of us have suffered consequences as a direct result of our denial. Examples include becoming unhappy and depressed while feeling like an imposter or a fake. Occasionally, this leads to self-destructive acts.

Depending on our circumstances, other influences can either act as catalysts or hindrances. A loving family can really help a gay person, while an unaccepting one can cause emotional damage. Unconditional love is taxed when a gay person comes out. If it's real, however, it soon shows itself. The church's hold on some of us was detrimental. According to some church doctrines, God offers only conditional love to humans. It took a great deal of courage for my co-researchers to challenge this dogma. Some still struggle with it.

What our friends thought of us was also important. Their influence could affect us either way. Mostly, they were helpful; thank God for loving friends. Other cultural influences could seriously hamper a gay person's ability to come out. For example, some Asian cultures have beliefs that are strongly opposed to the acceptance of gay people, a hindrance that had profound effect on Jonathan.

Deep in the psyche lies the seed of hope, and sooner or later we questioned our indoctrination into prejudice. Before a flame extinguishes, one last breath needs to be exhaled. If the breath is delicate enough, instead of blowing out, the candle burns with even greater intensity. Our flames began burning brightly as our spirits began making sense of the nonsense.

Eventually we were ready for our debut. Coming out to ourselves was the name of our debut, the next phase of our development. A new way of looking at life and living it was emerging.

Discussion Regarding These Experiences

The Catalysts

The catalysts inform homosexual males that they are gay. One of the first indicators is that nearly every homosexual boy feels different from other boys while growing up. This is a common theme both in the stories and in the published research. Many heterosexual boys also feel different from other kids for a variety of reasons, but these feelings are a typical part of maturing. Homosexual males often feel different during their childhood and adolescence for two additional reasons: (1) awareness of same-sex arousal and attraction and/or (2) development of cross-gender interests and traits.[12]

Cliff, for example, had felt different for both reasons. First, he described himself as a "nellie" child, having interests more typically experienced by females. This included greater interest in figure skating as opposed to hockey, and interest and participation in childhood cross-dressing.

Second, Cliff was aware of sexual interest in other males from age five. When he was seven or eight, he was actively checking out sixteen-to-twenty-year-olds in the locker room. His attraction and arousal toward the same gender was even further established by the beginning of his adolescence. He "owned a bunch of gay pornographic magazines" around that time and he soon became involved in a three-way relationship with a young gay couple.

Not everyone who is effeminate or develops cross-gender interests or traits is gay. Many heterosexual boys and men also exhibit these traits, which is one reason people often guess wrongly about someone's sexual orientation through observation of their dress or mannerisms. There are also innumerable gay men who are butch and masculine.

Gay men become aware of their sexual orientations by listening to what their minds and bodies are telling them. The same-sex messages may come through one or more channels, including (1) sexual arousal and attraction; (2) sexual fantasies and dreams; (3) falling in love; and (4) sexual acts.

Most youths who later self-define as gay initially experience same-gender sexual attractions and fantasies.[13] As Isay has suggested, "When homosexual impulses occur in a heterosexual adolescent, they usually are not manifest in behavior, but if they are, the sex is occasional, playful, without passion, and usually anxiety-ridden."[14] For the homosexual adolescent, the same-sex fantasies and impulses are both passionate and persistent.

For some, homosexual dreams become the segue to questioning one's sexual orientation. For example, Matthew planned to pursue his dream of becoming a Mennonite Minister. His conscious dream, however, was betrayed by subconscious dreams in his sleep, revealing explicit homosexual content. Isay clarified that it is erotic fantasy that defines the homosexual and not his behavior, because social constraints may inhibit some homosexuals, like some heterosexuals, from expressing their sexuality."[15] In essence, the intensity and frequency of an individual's sexual fantasies and dreams can be a guiding light toward self-identification as gay. The question becomes one of readiness—when to listen and act upon its illumination.

Many gay men become aware of their sexual orientation because of finding that they form either incomplete or unsatisfying connections with women. This lack of connection can occur either physically or emotionally, but both generally occur. Peter discovered that his heart did not go out to women. Although he loved his ex-wife, he never *fell* in love with her. This lack of romantic connection also translated into becoming detached during sexual activities. His mind would be elsewhere.

To love someone is different from *falling* in love. They might seem similar, but the difference is great. Most of us love our parents and our dearest friends. Gay fathers generally have the deepest love for their children. This love is filled with caring and commitment. The love that erupts with passion and blossoms with caring and commitment is romantic, consummate love,[16] and there is no comparison. Most men who identify as gay men have never had this experience with a woman, but most have had this experience with another man.

Sexual activity is another catalyst that helps foster coming out. A well-known gay theorist wrote that "it is sexual activity that most often prompts the eventual creation of homosexual identity."[17] In the "Coming Out" section of this book, Gavin revealed that sexual activity was an important part of his self-definition as gay. He stated that, "By the third or fourth time we were together, I decided that being gay was more my speed than being straight…I knew that this wasn't a passing phase."

Gay men question their psyches and search their souls, which I call the Ainside journey," before arriving at a self-definition as gay. Matthew, for example, vacillated between listening to his feelings and listening to the teachings of the Mennonite faith. The questioning eventually led to his coming out. Glenn was unusual in that his homoerotic interests did not reportedly develop until he was in his late twenties. Unlike most gay males, he did not feel different from other children growing up either. Nonetheless, Glenn later entered a serious questioning phase.

Although Glenn mentioned that he "walked the tightrope" while deciding whether he would date men or women, his sexual orientation was no more a choice than it is for any other gay male. "Although I was extremely attracted to her [i.e., Sharon]," Glenn stated, "I was unable to take the relationship beyond the level of a very good friendship. I didn't understand why."

Besides the "inside journey" discussed above, most gay men also begin an "outside journey" before coming out, taking preliminary steps into the "gay world" to learn about it and to find out how well it fits for them. Gavin talked about frequenting a bar which included a gay clientele soon after he completed high school. Almost half of the gay adolescents and adults come to define themselves as gay through their exploration of the gay world.[18] Beyond the bar scene, other examples of this exploration include observing media portrayals of gay men, reading about homosexuality and gay culture or experience, pursuing gay eroticism, joining gay clubs or organizations, attending gay events, and having friendships with gays.

Many gay men find it necessary to relocate to live as out gay men.[19] This is often necessary when significant family members are homophobic. In the "Beyond Coming Out" section of this book, Andrew explains that he did not tell his parents until he had moved away from home, and in fact waited until he was twenty-six before telling them.

The Hindrances

The hindrances serve to suppress the affirming messages which inform the homosexual male that he might be gay. The worst hindrance is *internalized homophobia*. The antigay messages have been, and still are, so pervasive throughout society that they become ingrained, even by those who are gay—sometimes most intensely by those who are gay. Paul shut the door on his feelings as a younger man because of society's abhorrence of them, which he had himself internalized. Peter fell passionately in love with Bob, while simultaneously succumbing to feelings of despair and suicidal gestures. Why did something as beautiful as love need to create such pain? The many corollaries of internalized homophobia are arguably the biggest obstacles in developing a positive gay identity. Where self-love as a gay person is compromised, the hidden culprit is often a derivative of this form of self-punishment.

There are many ways that people avoid facing reality, and often these are unconscious to us at the time. *Denial* is a defense mechanism that occurs, for the most part, unconsciously. When our mind cannot deal with something it finds painful, one way for it to cope is to pretend that it doesn't exist. We call this denial. Alcoholics who cannot face the damage alcohol is causing in their lives are in denial of their problem. Similarly, gay people who keep turning their back on their feelings are attempting to deny that their feelings are real.

Closely related to denial is *minimization*. Minimization occurs when we know that something is real, but we minimize its importance. For example, many gay men know from a young age that they are sexually attracted to guys, but instead of facing their feelings, they convince themselves that their homosexual feelings are not important.

Not only have gay men belittled their own emotions, but others have inadvertently, for the most part, contributed to this minimization as well. When gay people are physically demonstrative about their feelings in public, like any heterosexual couple would be, they are frequently berated and accused of "flaunting" themselves by heterosexual onlookers.[20] David laments in the "Coming Out" section of this book that he cannot dance with guys at a school social, and his mother regrets that he will not be safe walking hand-in-hand with a future boyfriend. My co-researchers were commonly told "it's just a phase" by well-meaning friends, relatives, and professionals. Paul mentioned in his story that people in the 1950s and 1960s believed that homosexuals could change if they so desired, and this belief continues within certain professional mental health circles today.[21]

Homosexual *behavior* may be a phase for some people as they mature,[22] but to suggest flippantly that their *feelings* are a phase is to do them a grave injustice. This is the type of minimization that has kept many people stuck in the cobwebs of their closets. To compound the angst, for some who have broken free, their baby steps into gay identity have collided with the strident views of those who believe that gay people can change and become heterosexual. Especially in the past, gay men commonly sought out psychotherapy to get "cured" of their homosexuality. This so-called "reparative therapy," or conversion therapy, was with few exceptions unsuccessful.[23]

One way that closeted homosexual men deal with their emotional pain is by becoming overly involved in work activities. When this is done as a conscious act of trying to avoid dealing with one's feelings, it is called *distraction*. When the individual is unaware of the reasons underlying the frantic efforts to work compulsively, it is called *overcompensation*. The person's work overcompensates for deep-rooted feelings of personal inadequacy. Often such individuals achieve a great deal while overcompensating, but paradoxically feel like either losers or imposters.

"I didn't want to be gay in high school so I stayed busy with other stuff," explained Andrew. This is an example of distraction. Peter worked very hard without understanding the underlying reasons, which is an example of overcompensation.

Many gay men, especially before and sometimes soon after coming out to themselves (but some indefinitely), experience something I call *heterofacsimile*. Heterofacsimile is a gay person's conscious and unconscious efforts to become straight, and to appear straight. These attempts to be heterosexual often occur both verbally, such as in one's use of language, and nonverbally, such as in one's appearance and mannerisms.

Some gay men have tried so hard to be straight that they married and in some instances had children. Other examples of heterofacsimile include trying to fit in by dating and sleeping with women and playing macho sports to appear more masculine or heterosexual.

John revealed a few examples of his heterofacsimile in our interview: "...I became very conscious of my attraction to males. I dealt with that in general by suppressing it and leading a straight and conventional lifestyle...I think mostly what kept me in the closet was that I wanted to become a productive, successful member of society...It was also because of social standing. I decided I would get married."

Heterofacsimile has damaging consequences. In essence, it becomes a way of belittling certain aspects of oneself and others. Underlying heterofacsimile is the long-standing belief that gay is less than straight. Clearly heterosexist societies have imposed this belief on gay people. As such, homophobia is an example of the fact that the majority have commonly had trouble accepting or even tolerating differences displayed by any minority culture.

The more gay people believe that they are inherently inferior, the less positive their self-concept. It's that simple, and it's that debilitating.

Another hindrance that both heterosexual and homosexual individuals have honored for centuries is what I call the *code of silence*. Until recently, the media has largely ignored the gay population, and this has made it difficult for gay individuals to find positive gay role models.[24] Families have tended not to talk openly about gay people, and when discussed, the conversation usually has negative connotations.

Tragically, gay people themselves have been largely quiet. Usually the most homophobic individuals are those who claim they do not know any gay people. After coming out to my colleagues at work, one woman said that in twenty years of counseling, she had never encountered a gay individual. Odds are, gay people were simply uncomfortable disclosing to her.

Given that we represent at least ten percent of the population, everyone probably knows at least one gay person. Unfortunately, those who could benefit the most from knowing gay people—individuals who are still homophobic—are the ones least likely to be aware of it, simply because gay individuals don't feel safe disclosing to them.

Yet another hindrance to coming out is stereotypes. Stereotypes are common, sometimes even among gay people who have been out for many years. The image of a pedophile with "coke bottle glasses, a wrinkled raincoat" lingered in Peter's mind for years. With the help of other people's interpretations and misconceptions, Peter became convinced that this image was that of a homosexual.

The stereotypes launched against gay men have been generally very negative, and sometimes completely absurd. These stereotypes include such descriptors as "mentally ill, emotionally crippled, neurotic, sexually confused, promiscuous, unfulfilled, parentally fixated, unhappy, obsessed, lonely, depressed, incapable of relationships,"[25] undependable, overly strong libidos, defective genes,[26] narcissistic, shallow, overly critical of others,[27] effeminate, and overly talkative.[28]

Hetrick and Martin[29] provided some less commonly held beliefs about gay people in their book. In the past, for example, homosexuals were blamed for destroying civilizations, a well-respected sexologist reported they could not whistle, they apparently lacked body hair, they caused the Second World War and the American defeat in Vietnam, they were child molesters, and they could not form mature nonsexual friendships with either sex. They also supposedly caused anorexia nervosa and crime in the streets.[30]

Given such negative—and completely false—stereotypes, is it any wonder that homosexual people have had such difficulty in coming out, and that their families have not generally been joyous about their son's or daughter's news? Stereotypes have been a major obstacle for gay people, both before and during their coming out.

Many gay people have felt rejected by others, and others have been all too accommodating, especially in the past. Andrew was aware that he was gay from a young age, yet he decided to keep his feelings to himself. The cost was that Andrew felt isolated and alone throughout his adolescence. His sister had a difficult time of it as well. Andrew explained how their parents initially reacted by isolating her from the house. Feelings of isolation and rejection are common among gay adolescents,[31] who are oftentimes exasperated by having unsupportive parents.

Influences that Either Serve as Catalysts or Hindrances

Some influences can serve as either catalysts or hindrances. Family of origin is a good example. If the parents of a gay person are gay positive in their values and beliefs, this can tremendously assist their son's or daughter's coming out. As mentioned earlier, most families are shocked and have trouble accepting, at least initially, their gay son's or daughter's sexual orientation, which will cause difficulties for the gay child.

Peers are also an important influence. A young person's peer group provides the foundation for developing intimacy, autonomy, and self-esteem.[32] Consequently, supportive friends can greatly ease an individual's transition to a gay identity.

Another influence is that of the church. The Christian church is often criticized for having negatively affected society's acceptance of homosexuality. This is not universally the case today.[33] The United Church of Christ and the Metropolitan Community Church are two examples of modern Christian churches that are accepting of gay individuals. But most churches worldwide, Christian or otherwise, remain unaccepting of sexually active gay people.

Furthermore, society and culture also influence coming out, either positively or negatively. Jonathan was aware that Asian culture was unaccepting of his sexual identity; interestingly, same-gender relations were accepted in ancient China.[34] This continued until the twentieth century, when the prevailing view concerning homosexuality changed to one labeling it "moral degeneracy."[35]

Jonathan speaks about not fulfilling the "obligations of an Oriental grandson." He believed—along with other family members—that he would not have children, particularly sons, to pass on the family name. Many gay couples today seriously consider the possibility of having children, either through adoption (where permissible by law) or through co-parenting with a member of the opposite sex. The available research on this topic supports what most gay people already know in their hearts: gay people are generally very loving and yes, they make excellent parents.[36] Furthermore, their sexual orientation does not "rub off" on their children.[37] If the children are straight, they will be straight. If they are homosexual, they will hopefully accept their feelings and come out. Child rearing practices do not determine sexual orientation.

Societal influence also affected Jerome's coming out, but unlike Jonathan's, the particular African culture where Jerome lived was more positive and accepting of homosexuality and sexuality in general compared to Western society. The contrast helped him question his own sexual orientation, which helped foster his eventual self-acceptance.

Chapter Five
Coming Out Stories

Matthew, 32

My friends from university and I discussed topics like racism, feminism, and homosexuality. I learned from these talks that it doesn't matter if you're gay. I developed a mostly positive view of homosexuals, although I was still afraid of them. There was no judgment from my friends, and I began to believe that it was okay to be gay. That made it okay for me to come out to myself, and I didn't hate myself because I was gay. I think there were still many things to overcome, but ideologically I didn't have a problem with gay people or being gay. Guilt was what I had to get over first in order to come out, so that was very important.

My attraction to males increased in third year, when I became involved in various student productions. I became more active in theater, and rehearsals were often on Sunday mornings. I stopped going to church and pulled away from other Christian groups as rehearsals occurred throughout the week. In my third year, I smoked a cigarette for the first time because it was part of a role that I was doing. It also represented a lessening of the church's hold on me and the beginning of finding myself—like doing things that I wasn't supposed to do. In theater, I had a license to do the things that I wasn't supposed to do, because I wasn't being myself, I was playing another role. That was thrilling, and it whetted my appetite for other things.

I began questioning what was wrong with smoking and drinking. I went to a cast party and had a couple of glasses of champagne. I felt bad about that, but I also enjoyed the thrill immensely of having this take over my body. I had no tolerance at all and I felt looped. Another time, I got totally smashed out of my mind with scotch.

In April, I directed my first major play. I picked a play by Joe Orton, who is a famous gay playwright from London, and I started to study him and read his diaries. It was the first time I read about someone who was openly gay. I read about all the sexual practices that he engaged in with his lovers, and he became a hero to me. The play that I produced wasn't overtly gay, but it had many gay overtones in it.

At the end of the play I called up John, a guy who starred in the play, and I asked him out for coffee. I decided that I was going to come out to him, and I hoped that something could happen between us. We went out for coffee and chatted, and then when I drove him home, I told him. I'm sure I scared the shit out of him. I let him know that I was interested in spending time with him, and he made it clear that he wasn't. I felt terribly rejected and wondered if I was completely unattractive. Why doesn't he want to be with me? I'm a nice person. At this point, I admitted to myself that I was gay.

After third year, I traveled throughout Manitoba as part of a drama tour. Martin was also on this tour, and although he was straight, I fell in love with him. He was a classically beautiful man, and we got along really well. We had done several plays together in my third year, which is when I first became attracted to him.

That summer we spent considerable time together. He smoked, I smoked. He drank, I drank. I experienced more fun than I ever had before; I was finally part of the group. I wasn't living by anyone's laws or standards, and I felt incredibly free.

I knew I couldn't come out until I worked through my spiritual journey. Friends challenged my religious beliefs. For example, they asked "Why is what you're doing any different from what I'm doing? Why do you think you'll go to heaven and I won't go to heaven?"

A major shift in my religious outlook and my thinking about it was occurring. I didn't feel accepted at church and I didn't feel a part of it. I didn't believe the same things anymore. I thought everyone was quite narrow and not willing to explore. I also felt guilty, however, because of my spirituality, not my sexuality. "What if I'm wrong in thinking that Christianity isn't right? If it is right, then I'm on a road to hell."

After I returned from that tour, I decided to give Christianity one last chance. That same summer was the one hundredth anniversary of the Mennonite Brethren in Canada, and I left on a youth mission. I felt like such a hypocrite, but I was really open and honest with people. I told people that I was going through a crisis and questioning the validity of my beliefs. The further I got into it, the more I had no time for it. My attitude sucked, and I couldn't wait to get home.

The summer ended, and I moved in with Martin, who had asked

me if I wanted to be his roommate. I think my parents were concerned about why I would want to leave home. I think they knew something was going on. That autumn I rejected Christianity. I began partying a lot, went to bars a lot, and I was very involved with theater.

I started dating a good female friend of Martin's. I thought my biggest problem was that I had never slept with a woman, which was one of the main reasons why I dated her. We fooled around, but we always stopped short of having sex. One night we were naked together, and we necked, petted, and I stimulated her with my fingers. She gave me a blow job, but nothing happened. I felt really frustrated and guilty because I couldn't come. It dawned on me that I wasn't physically attracted to her. We broke up shortly after New Year's 1989.

Martin was dating a woman named Susan at that point, and I was supremely jealous of their relationship. My relationship with Martin subsequently disintegrated, and we developed significant animosity toward each other. I think we miscommunicated about many things. Eventually, he and Susan moved out.

My first attractions for men were mostly physical, but I wanted something emotional as well. I still had not been in love with someone who requited it. I had fallen in love with Martin, but I felt let down by him.

In August 1989, I phoned the gay line at the university and I talked to a guy there for several hours on the telephone. We arranged a meeting, I went to his place, and we talked until two in the morning. The third time we got together, we went to the bar. This was my first time, and I was very nervous. One of the first people I saw there was someone I knew, and I sank into the corner, hoping he wouldn't see me. I was really embarrassed, but later, I started hanging out with that guy. His name was Frank, and he was seeing a guy named Peter. They became my first gay friends.

One night I went out and met this really hot guy who was rumored to be a porn star from San Francisco. I watched him, and then we started talking. We went out to my car and smoked some hash. It really freaked me out when he put his hand on my lap. We later had another toke and eventually went to my place and smoked more. I was ready to burst sexually, and he became my first sexual partner. I forget much of that whole experience, but I remember coming, and I felt like I had a fucking geyser coming out of me. It was such a relief. Later, I felt freaked out by the experience. I didn't feel guilt, however. I knew I wanted more of this.

The second time I had sex was with a guy who wanted to fuck me. We attempted it, but it was far too painful. It wasn't a positive experience. The next weekend, I went over to the house of an older guy who was interested in me. My friends and I had talked to him at the bar and although I wasn't really interested in him, I craved attention from males. He started caressing me, and I ended up being on his bed. As he began undressing me, I started thinking, I don't want to be here, I don't want this to happen. I had to fight him off. It almost turned into date rape.

That event changed things for me. I made a decision that although I was gay, it didn't mean that my life necessarily had to change. My focus would not be going to the bar every weekend. My gay identity doesn't need to be out there somewhere; it can be within who I am already, and I don't have to change all aspects of myself to be gay. That summer I told three friends that I was gay, and I remember talking about it with another person.

I returned to university to finish my degree in the fall of 1989. I still went out periodically, maybe once a month on average. I didn't have many sexual partners or even many gay friends. I didn't really find it happening in the small city where I lived, and I was busy at school. At that point, my theater lifestyle was separate from my gay lifestyle because I was not widely out yet. I didn't have any gay friends that were really serious about anything or that had any depth to them. My gay life had emerged as a shallow experience.

In 1990, I was in Vancouver during the Olympic Gay Games and I met this really interesting guy from Boston. We chatted for a long time and I realized that there were some really nice gay men out there. Meeting him was an important experience for me. I also went to a dance where there were over one thousand gay men, and it was really exciting.

I finished university in the winter of 1991 and I dated one guy for a while, but it wasn't meaningful. I became disillusioned. I think at that point I had only been with three other guys sexually before, and now this one. My self-image was still fairly negative. For example, I didn't feel that I was attractive and I didn't feel that talented in the theater group either.

Peter, 40

After nattering at my therapist for the first half hour, he said I struck him as a man who's ready to take his own life. I stopped. No one had ever confronted me with that question. I mean I knew about my self-destructive behavior, but I didn't view it as suicidal. Once it dawned on me that I was suicidal, it was a real struggle to continue living. I would look at those razor blades and I would look at those pills, and it was tempting. I would not allow it to break me, however, as I always had a strong spirit. I had two choices—either kill myself or see if there was another alternative. It was just that I felt so much pain in not doing something that I did do something.

After this first visit with my psychologist, my wife and I decided to part ways for reasons unrelated to my emerging sexuality. We agreed to separate on a trial basis, because we were both unhappy and we were going in different directions. I didn't want to drag her down with what I felt would become a tumultuous event in my life. Furthermore, I didn't want her to see me fail. I had never failed in anybody's eyes, and I felt that I was just about ready to lose it. I didn't want anybody to see it. She was going through similar issues as well, and later accepted her own homosexuality. We had been high school sweethearts, so we found something in common with each other. We were probably then both harbouring gay feelings.

My therapist felt from day one that I was gay. I would start talking about Bob and losing him and I would start sobbing. He knew I was in love with him. He slowly started planting the seed that healthy gay people are people that you wouldn't spot on the street as any different from anyone else. After about eight months of therapy, I finally came to the conclusion that I was in a gay relationship.

My life became completely dismantled during the two years of therapy. I had left the warmth and security of a marriage, and I dropped the multitude of friends who used me because of my power and financial success. They were not going to tolerate me changing the "always obliging, always successful, never failing, always helpful, always-will-carry-me-if-I-need-to-be-carried" type of person that I had been up to that point. The only way I could come out and see what I wanted was to stop associating with the people who wanted me to be what they wanted. That was probably the most traumatic part of my coming out and developing a positive gay identity—there were so many people whom I would disappoint. There was also a total dismantling of relationships with my family. Nobody liked the changes that were happening.

During my therapy, I became a voracious reader, and I picked up every reputable, modern book on homosexuality. The first thing I had to do was rid myself of the negative images and the stereotypes. I needed to put a face on healthy gay people. I read a study conducted by a Chicago polling firm that surveyed Americans living in different parts of the United States. The people that were most homophobic, that had the most virulently hateful views about gay people were also the same people who did not believe that they knew any gay people.

This demonstrated to me that it's much easier to hate a group if they don't have a face. The minute you know your neighbor or your daughter or your son or your mailman or your butcher is gay, if you like that person, you've suddenly got a real dilemma to confront. Once I began to accept that I could, in fact, be a normal person and not adopt a bunch of affectations and unhealthy behavior and stuff like that, coming out became possible. Toward the end of the therapy, I felt strong enough to step down from my prestigious, high-powered job, and I resigned.

Frank, 38

My experience in Florida led me to identify as gay. I had made the transition. There were times even after I came out to myself that I had an experience with another woman or two, but they were aware that I was gay.

I didn't have to correct any stereotypes in my thinking. I wasn't exposed to much discussion or information about what being gay was or what the stereotypes of being gay were before coming out. Consequently, there weren't too many things that I had to overcome. As kids, people call you a sissy or a faggot or cocksucker or whatever they say, but it meant nothing to me. It was no different from calling someone any derogatory name that has no meaning to someone who's really young. Eventually somebody tells you what being a fag means. As you get older, you're watching the news coverage and you see dykes on bikes and the Sisters of Perpetual Indulgence in the parades and stuff like that. I never felt that all gay people dressed up in dresses or wore wigs. I never had any real stereotypes like that.

The only stereotype I would have had is that gay people have some effeminate characteristics. I still believe that most effeminate men are probably gay.

The first relationship that I had was with a guy named Brad, and that lasted for about six months. It was predominantly a sexually based relationship, I believe. My sister found out that I was dating him through a work associate. She came home and told my mother. Mom said, "Your sister has told me some very disturbing news, and I want you to tell me what's going on." So I told her.

Before this event, I guess I had some questions about the normality of being gay. I had gone on my own to see a psychiatrist, and I had a very interesting chat with him. He was asking me questions like, "Well, do you have any difficulty socializing? Do you have any trouble sleeping? Do you have health issues surrounding your being gay?" All of my answers were no. He said, "Well, you really don't have a problem of a psychological nature whatsoever. If you're thinking that being gay is a mental illness, it's not. If you're having any problems accepting yourself being gay, then you've got a problem to discuss."

After my mother found out, her first reaction was, "We should get you to a psychiatrist or a psychologist." She worked in the medical community and knew the doctor that I had seen. He's reputable, so she thought about it longer, and her main concern became my happiness and my health. She was concerned that growing up without the love of children would be a hardship to me in future years, and she was also aware of the societal problems that I might experience, but she was very loving, caring, compassionate, and understanding. I was lucky to have that type of nurturing mother relationship.

Gavin, 32

After completing high school in 1982, I returned to my parents' home. I started frequenting a bar which was probably 60% gay. I also went to another bar occasionally where the patrons were mostly gay. Walking into a bar for the first time was nerve-racking. I didn't grow up in a bar culture, and this was also out of my community and my lifestyle. I was fairly attractive and young, and I remember thousands of eyes staring at me. It was really intimidating.

I started hanging around with a woman there, and one night her boyfriend invited me to come over to his place. I thought, "this sounds fine," and since he had a girlfriend, I felt comfortable. We ended up at his place, and we started to kiss. Then my shirt came off, and his shirt came off, and he gave me oral sex. I felt uncomfortable. By the third or fourth time we were together, I decided that being gay was more my speed than being straight. It happened quickly. It was a time, too, when there were a lot more gay people in the media. I knew that this wasn't a passing phase. Our encounters went on for two or three months.

I had my first sexual encounter with a woman when I was eighteen. I thought it was about time to give this a whirl, but it wasn't really a good experience. I was uncomfortable and I didn't understand how it was supposed to work. I've had one other experience with a woman who knew I was gay, but she had a massive crush on me. She insisted that we have sex, and I finally complied. It was fine, actually.

I decided to move back to Vancouver in the fall of 1983 to prevent embarrassing my teachers, neighbors, and family. I hadn't told anybody yet that I was gay, other than my closest friends. I also figured that this move would give me more freedom to be gay. I stayed there for about six months.

Subsequently, I decided to move back to my home city and fess up to my family and friends. I was completely prepared to be written out of everyone's life and my family's will. The desire to tell them was so strong in me that I decided that if they don't love me because I'm a fag, then that's fine.

Upon my return, I asked my mom and my two sisters to meet me at a neutral place. I told them I was gay and that I wanted everyone to go away and think about this. My mom told one of her closest friends about our meeting, and his response was, "Is that it?" She then read some books on the subject. She was completely fine with it from day one.

My dad lived about a block away from my mom. He knew that I was going to gay bars, so I think he knew, but he was diagnosed with Alzheimer's soon after I got back from Vancouver. I decided it wasn't worth telling him, and as it turned out, he deteriorated very quickly. I really don't think he would have reacted positively to it.

I met a fellow by the name of Ken and we became good friends.

He saw potential in me and decided that he would take me under his wing. He purchased two adjoining gay bars and made me the manager of both. I had absolutely no experience, but he trusted that I could wing it. I was nineteen at the time. I had such huge responsibilities, yet I looked and was so young. I developed a protectionist snotty air that I still have in a gay bar. I become unapproachable.

I walked home with a friend one night down a street which was known as part of the hustler strip. We were talking outside his apartment when a car load of staff from the bar drove by. The driver slammed on his brakes, they looked at me and said, "Oh my God, that's Gavin!" They thought I was trying to pick up a hustler, and from that day forward they had much less respect for me.

I learned in my childhood not to have sex until I'm married. The idea of having multiple sexual partners never interested me. I was looking at finding a true love, rather than just a sexual experience, so I never got into that part of the gay culture. I didn't want a bunch of guys to know me sexually because that would give them the potential to gossip. After my experience of being on thirteenth avenue, I was never going to allow it to happen again.

I managed the bars for about three months before Ken lost the business. He subsequently went into another business and convinced me to do the same. We ended up being successful in our business partnership.

Jonathan, 30

Between ages twelve and fourteen, I thirsted for knowledge about being gay. I read about the gay life in San Francisco and I learned that gays were concentrated mainly in big cities. I read a lot about gay people: their behavior and their lifestyle. Because I read mostly magazines, my concept of gay life when I was younger was the club scene where guys danced half-naked. I found this image exciting and glamorous.

I told a few female friends in grade ten that I was gay. All the people I chose to tell became supportive and thought it was cool. I never came out to a male friend except my best friend, who is himself gay. He started giving me pamphlets about the gay and lesbian community center here and then he eventually took me out to the bar. I was involved with sports, and there were social clubs and the students' union, so I had high profile. I really didn't get hassled much. I never told the people that I knew would give me problems.

In high school, as in any grade, you get the same ridicule no matter whether you are gay or not. You get picked on simply for being different in your appearance or your behavior. I was never afraid that others would find out I was gay. I was concerned for my friends, however, in that they might get ridiculed for hanging around a gay person.

Emotionally I was never attracted to women. I liked the emotional support they provided but it wasn't an emotional bond that I wanted from them. There was no sexual bond at all. I certainly have not had a lack of beautiful women in my life. They were always around me. Beautiful women still turn my head, but I don't notice them in a sexual way. I appreciate them aesthetically.

My family moved around almost once a year, usually to a small town. It's really hard to find gay identity when you're living in a small town because you can't blend in and there are few people you can discuss it with or tell. Shortly after we moved to Calgary where I would begin grade nine, Dad announced that we would be moving again. I put my foot down with my father and I told him I would stay in Calgary. I finally took a stance and said this is what I want. My brother and I stayed in a one-bedroom apartment, and I took care of him. My parents returned after a year or so and we again lived together.

That's when the confrontation started. I started going out to the bars in grade ten and eleven. A couple of times I stayed out later than my curfew. The last time I broke it was pretty severe because they locked me out. I had to sleep in the hallway of the apartment until they allowed me to reenter.

I was a good child and always honest with my parents. I usually got what I wanted because I was rational and responsible. Consequently, my parents often let me stay out later than my curfew.

I started going to gay bars at age sixteen. The sea of men was incredible, but at such a young age, it was really hard to get picked up. I have no idea why. That was a bad time in my gay life, when I was coming out. It wasn't that I didn't feel good about myself but it was the projection that I didn't feel good about myself because other people wouldn't notice me. I felt a lot of depression, and it made me question my happiness about being gay.

I think we all face doubt when we are unhappy at a certain stage. I thought maybe if I tried being straight I could find some happiness. It wasn't that I actually questioned being gay, but I wondered if the gay thing would go away and if I would find happiness if I got married. Happiness was my one and only driving force: it wasn't directly about being gay.

It was pretty rough for about eighteen months. I had to deal with the fact that I was a minority as far as being gay because there were no other Chinese gay people that I met. That was really hard because when you go to the bar and you're young, you want to be picked up, you want to be liked, and when it doesn't happen, you look for answers. One answer I surmised was that maybe these guys aren't into Orientals. I knew I was not the only gay person, but I soon realized there were few gay Oriental people living in Calgary. I felt like I was right back at square one, which was difficult.

I had a very negative sexual experience when I was sixteen. I thought I wanted to go all the way with this older man, but I said *no* in the middle of it, and there was no going back. I ended up being forced into anal sex. My friend took me down to the community center for gay people, and we talked to a counselor. I was embarrassed because I didn't want anybody to know.

One night I was fortunate enough to pick up a guy, but there was a condition attached to it. He wanted my best friend, Don, to join us. I'm thinking "Whoa, this is my first experience and it's going to be harsh—a threesome with my best friend." The experience became one-sided, because this guy really just wanted my best friend.

Afterwards, Don went home, and I stayed the night. I wanted that affection so much, that man-to-man affection, that warm, pseudolove. I knew the consequences, you know, I knew I had a curfew, I knew everything. I wasn't drunk, I wasn't on drugs or anything.

I took the bus home that morning feeling really depressed because the experience had been so empty. Everything I had wished for the night before was not the next day. The sex hadn't been gratifying, and there was an absence of affection.

As I was arriving home, my parents were preparing to leave. I told them in Chinese that I'm gay. It was really weird because I hadn't rehearsed it, and I never even dreamed of telling them. Suddenly the whole world just turned black and caved in. They began yelling at the top of their lungs and I began yelling as well. I yelled at my father, "I'm this way because of you!" The slap across my face ended the conversation.

The next week was just hell. My mom stayed in her bedroom bawling her head off. I would come home and go to my room. That's it. There was dead silence between us. I had had enough by the following weekend, and I decided to go to the bar again. My parents asked, "Where are you going?" I replied, "I'm just going out to the bar." That was all that was said. As I was nearly finished getting ready, my father came out and said, "If you love us you will stay home from now on and not go to these places. If you walk out this door tonight, don't ever come back." That was an easy decision for some kid who's seventeen and rebellious. So I said, "Okay, thank you," and I closed the door and left. I didn't come home that night. The next day I asked Don to pick me up, and I moved out. I lived on my own for four years.

I understand how shocking the news was to my parents. That's society's fault for separating the homosexual from the heterosexual. If you look at the heterosexual society and the homosexual society, they are very similar. We go shopping, we go to movies, we get married, we get divorced, we go to hospitals, we do everything.

A year after I moved out, my parents proceeded to get a divorce. My mother discovered my father was having the third or fourth affair within five or six years, and she had had enough. I felt total hatred toward my father for what he did to my mother. To this day I'm still angry. When I see him, my temper flares immediately. I haven't seen him for over a year. Perhaps I still resent him for throwing me out when I was younger. My father has often tried to reconcile by asking me out for dinner, but I always refuse. Most of my anger, however, is because he left my mom as a divorcee. She's alone in her house. He's caused her so much pain over the years. I've always wanted stability in my life, and my father never gave us that. He's always been a heavy gambler and we always moved.

Jerome, 48

Although I consciously denied or pretended that I wasn't gay, I started seeking more information. By this time there was a freeing up in the general media. Movies and television were presenting gay characters periodically, but most of it was pretty negative.

I started spending time in areas where men cruise, not in bars but in outdoor areas where there were cars. I soon began cruising as well. At the time, I was terrified of people finding out. I enjoyed the sex, however, and had no difficulty thinking that it was bad or anything.

I met a fellow that I got to know, and I became infatuated with him. He was a great deal more accepting of his sexuality and much more aware of being gay than I was, which to some extent was frightening for me. One of the few regrets I have is that I wasn't ready for a relationship then, and I really closed it off. I accepted a job in another city, and I didn't tell him. I was still ignoring what my feelings were telling me. I wanted to be seen as straight, and part of my motivation was because I was teaching young kids and didn't want to be outed. For some years, this fear pushed me into leading two different lives: one at work and the other that was involved sexually with men. I kept the two lives entirely apart and hoped they would never cross. My friends were still almost exclusively heterosexual.

When I moved, I found out fairly quickly where the gay bars were, and although I didn't actually go to the bars, I went near them to meet other men for primarily sexual purposes. I enjoyed the sex and the intimacy that came with it at the time, but I was not desiring intimacy from a gay relationship. I was afraid of it. I had a lot of social interaction, which provided for my intimacy needs. I always overworked, partly because I believed I had to do more or better work than straight men.

Some time later, I attended graduate school, and there was a large active gay and lesbian community there. I did not become involved in it, but I knew about it. I became roommates again with Joe, who was actively involved in a gay relationship. He had several gay friends that he spent time with, and his social circle was clearly becoming gay.

The first time I went to a gay bar, I went alone. I cased out the place several times before I could enter. It was both exciting and terrifying. It was probably a step into beginning to consciously acknowledge that I was gay as opposed to ignoring it. I went to a couple of other gay bars afterwards, where it was easier to chat with people, as opposed to this place, which was a noisy dance bar.

I soon met a fellow with whom I had a brief, intense fling, and I finally acknowledged that I was gay and I began talking about it to him. I was still doing a lot of reading and trying to keep up with what was happening in the gay world.

Later, I established my first relationship, which lasted for a couple years. I was still in the closet at work and with straight people and it became more complicated trying to hide my lover. My two lives were beginning to grate on me.

I was still concerned about how my immediate family would react. I knew from others that it could be a negative experience, and my family was fairly religious. I was also afraid what people at work would think. I was still working with young kids, and I was concerned that they would assume I was a pedophile. I felt vulnerable. I also resented having to keep my worlds separate.

I think many changes were happening for me as my identity consolidated. I moved to another city in 1980 to begin a job teaching students in an early childhood program. I became immersed with work, and I was just busy like mad. One thing that I thought about when I moved was that I wanted to get involved in the gay community. It didn't happen, however, as I wasn't there long enough, and my job took too much time and energy.

After a couple years, I moved again to work for a provincial government as an Early Childhood Development Consultant. One of my goals was to become involved with the gay and lesbian community, and the first people I started to get to know outside work were gay individuals.

I went to a western gay and lesbian conference on a weekend, and this became the first gay activity that I ever attended. I met many people and found out more about the other gay organizations. The conference was exciting and I enjoyed participating in it. They had a little march, which I wasn't brave enough to join, but watching it was important to me, as I felt closer to being public.

The seminal event for me was a bathhouse raid, because I was there that night. I had lived in the city less than a year when it happened. The police came charging in, and I was arrested along with everybody else. Truthfully, I was watching television at the time. I knew about earlier raids that had occurred in Toronto and Montreal, but I remember feeling both helpless and angry with myself for not really knowing the law, my rights, and the implications of this arrest. We were all charged with being found at a bawdy house under the criminal code. I said to myself that I would never let that happen again.

Even if I had been involved sexually with men there, the fact that we were all treated like criminals seemed insane to me. I began moving in some different directions real fast after that night ended. When I eventually got home, there were big headlines in the newspaper. I telephoned a gay organization and was told to come down because they were having a meeting. There were media all over the place. A bigger meeting was held at the local gay bar later, and the media wanted to talk to people who were present the night of the raid.

I had dealt with the media in my professional life, and I decided to talk with them. The first thing the media asked me was what name I wanted to use, and the only one I could think of was my own! Television and radio used my live voice, and several people told me afterward that I have a fairly distinctive voice, and they had figured out my identity.

On Monday I went to work a little worried, but I also didn't think anyone would know. I was certainly concerned, as I was dealing with kindergarten programs in the region. The people I worked with in smaller communities became aware that I was gay, because the bathhouse raid was the biggest story around for a couple weeks. It was in the newspapers and broadcast over radio throughout the province.

A couple of people I knew through work were supportive. Others told me they were really proud of the way I handled it. Some said the fact that I'm gay was fine with them and that they expected to continue working with me as they always had. There were some others who found it difficult and offensive, but that's life. I never look back in that regard. By comparison, I can't believe I lived my earlier years in the closet.

Reporters were after me again, wanting to write more articles about me, and I decided either I was going to do it and use my name or I wasn't going to do it. It was one or the other, and I decided I would do it and use my name, and I've never changed since then. It turned out that I was the only one who would talk. That, for me, was really dealing with my sexuality publicly. I was no longer worried if some people wouldn't like me because of being gay. I had enough friends who did accept me as I am. I realize that this sounds easier than it was. It did take some time to work through this and rebuild my confidence, but I never again denied I was gay.

Fréderic, 38

My dad died in 1980, and I moved to Montreal the same year to work on a degree in history. Montreal was mecca. The first day I went to the bar, however, I could have been a wall or a table; I wanted to hide because I was frightened. I didn't know any of these people. Also, gay bars tend to be dark, smoky places with loud music—we're not talking about a Monet painting with blue skies and flowers. Some bars even specialize in looking like dungeons. I often went by myself and consequently made another step toward having greater independence. I had several one-night stands, but I didn't develop a long-term relationship. I never have, in fact.

I developed a friendship with the world while I was in Montreal. I knew then that to be a positive gay person is not to be stuck in a gay ghetto. Instead, it is to be with the world. My sense of a gay community wasn't made with walls; it was made with flowers and bridges that would reach people. I think life is about mixing people together as much as you can.

I spent three years in Montreal. I joined the university gay association there and developed a group of gay friends. There were about six of us. We talked about men and going out with men, we went to gay bars together, and we planned dances. We felt that being gay was about serving the community and helping the community to grow. That period of university was very meaningful to me, and I still have deep feelings for these friends.

My second eldest gay brother, Guy, had recently finished a degree and lived with my mother for a few years. I think he took advantage of her financially. His actions were also disrespectful. Instead of being sincere with her about his gayness, he acted flippantly. I found that hurtful, because Mom developed more hatred about being gay. I had to face her with coming out, and it was a horrible experience. My mom was a person who lived with gay sons but didn't speak about it. It was a nonexisting lifestyle to her.

One fall, my mother visited me and discovered a gay magazine. At lunchtime, she brought the magazine to the table and asked, "What's this?" That was after Dad's death, so she added, "Dad would oppose that. What are you doing with that magazine?" My mom was on the attack, and I was on the defensive. She had read an article in that magazine about a priest who abused a child, which fed her disgusting view regarding homosexuality. I told her that I had sexual desire for men, and she was horrified. The only images she had of gay people were purely negative. For her it was linked to sins like adultery and promiscuity. She is a profound Catholic, and she used to be a nun before she married. From that day forward, I knew it wasn't going to be talked about again. Mom didn't speak to me for three days.

The idea that I was gay became clearer when I moved to CEJEP, which is a two-year college in Quebec. I was twenty, and I was away from family. I met two friends there that were gay. One of my teachers was gay, and we became friends too. When I moved to CEJEP, I thought that I was going to be rejected because of my gayness. I told my friend Bonnie, "If I tell you three words, I will lose all my friends." I ending up telling her. I said, "I am gay," and she said, "You've not lost me." At that moment, I became more gay-positive, emotionally. I became unwilling to accept people who would not accept my gayness.

Tommy, 41

During my second year of university, I accepted myself as a gay person and came out of the closet. I never had any ambivalence about being gay, as my sexual fantasies were always with males. I started telling people that I was gay, and it felt great. I had some meetings with people at the local gay information service, and I started accepting myself more and met some gay people. I became focused on meeting a guy my own age and having a relationship. I remember reading a positive book about homosexuality and homosexual experience written by Tripp. Positive books like this one were uncommon in those days.

During that period of time three of us formed the first gay organization at the university. We put up posters in gay bars and at the gay information service. The three of us created our own peer group this way, and we became assertive about our gay identity. We weren't afraid to be seen putting up gay posters and suffer stigmatization. On one occasion we put up posters in the morning and later noticed that they had been torn down. We followed the trail and found the culprit. I jumped him and we began fighting, which created quite a disturbance. Although such experiences were struggle-oriented, they gelled my identity, and that was positive. During that period, I wanted everybody in my personal world to know I was gay.

To develop a positive gay identity, I needed to alter the negative stereotypes of gay people. The term "gay" was derogatory, and it implied being less of a human being, or "sick." Who would want to be gay if this were true? I needed to accept the fact that I was gay and appreciate its legitimacy: that it was okay, that it was fine. I should clarify that my low self-esteem was not simply the result of being gay. There were several other issues too.

As I began to declare my gayness to the world, that was liberating and helpful to my self-esteem. It represented a self-accepting attitude that said, I'm no longer hiding, I'm not ashamed, and it's okay to have sex and fall in love with men.

I fell in love with Michael, who was one of the founders of our gay organization. That was a significant relationship, which lasted for a couple of years. My gay identity felt pretty secure during that period. When we broke up, however, I went through a strong emotional crisis. I stopped pursuing a committed relationship for years. Partly I was afraid, and partly I lost confidence when this relationship ended. I felt like a failure.

Cliff, 30

When I was twelve or thirteen, I owned a bunch of gay pornographic magazines. I knew that this was okay because if it was bad, there wouldn't be so many magazines and books on the market. My frustration was that I couldn't do anything about it, as none of the sexual stuff ever happened to me. Although I had heard of other kids having sexual experiences during sleepovers, I never did, because I knew what I was and I knew that I didn't want to ruin a friendship. I wasn't attracted to any of them either. They weren't my type, as I've always been attracted to older men.

My dad is a retired construction worker, and with a grade six or grade seven education, he became a self-made millionaire. He was an alcoholic and both emotionally and physically abusive. I remember a few times where he had friends over late at night, and he would wake us from sleep to do push-ups for his friends, and then one arm push-ups, until we were exhausted.

He beat up on all of us at home. I moved to Calgary with my aunt and cousins when I was thirteen because I thought I was to blame for his abusiveness. I was different, which frustrated him, and he didn't know how to react to me.

I was also smoking marijuana and going through a turbulent adolescence. I was a bad, rotten teenager: crabby and skipping school. I was mixed up, and I had to go because both of my parents were having trouble handling me. I thought everything would be okay if I left. Dad became even more abusive to the others at home, however. Although he's now mellowed, he's still crabby.

When I was fourteen, I was sitting at a bus stop and a van pulled up with two guys in it. They asked me if I wanted a ride. They were both smiling and very good-looking and I thought, "Hmm, sure I'll take a ride." They were in their twenties, and they were lovers. I didn't know that at the time, though. They dropped me off and suggested that I call them for a ride back after I finished visiting my friend. I did.

They took me over to their place, and we smoked a couple of joints. We started having sex, and I ended up staying with them until I was seventeen years old. They were a couple and I was the third, but they never made me feel like I wasn't welcome. They loved each other, and I was with both of them equally. It was great. Both had varied interests and both were different from each other. One was an auto mechanic, while the other was an artist. The artist was very creative and turned me on to many different types of music. Another difference was that one was more effeminate and the other was more butch. I think I brought them something they didn't have, or we wouldn't have been together that long. In some ways, I was their kid.

I eventually moved out from living with these guys because they were moving to Vancouver. I met a photographer when I was eighteen or nineteen, and I became his assistant. I went with him to Regina for six months, and then he took me to Saskatoon. Although we related to each other sexually, it didn't last long. He was a thirty-five-year-old baby.

Paul, 50

In November 1985, I decided that I could not continue living this way—as a married man pretending to be heterosexual—but I still didn't want anyone to know the reason. What changed my whole life and made me accept myself was the night I planned suicide. I left no notes, no letters, no nothing, so that no one would know it was suicide. After getting the car up to 160 miles-per-hour, I began driving it off the road when I heard a voice say, "No, Paul, you have more to live for." I changed my mind, readjusted my car on the road, and stopped.

I realized that I do have more to live for. Why should I end and destroy my life because of what society thinks? From that moment on I decided that I'm going to be who I am and I won't care what people think of me anymore. They can either be my friend or not, but it's going to be their gain or their loss and that became my attitude. I finally rid myself of the vicious stereotypes that I was raised with regarding gay people. It basically happened over night. By the time I came to that point I had already dealt with a lot of that shit and I was ready to be free.

At that point I was also involved in a gay relationship with Tony, another married man. My relationship with him had started ten years earlier. My ex-wife had an affair two years after we were married and I was beginning to get over that and forgive her when she had a second one. That's when I met Tony.

I thought this clandestine relationship would work out well because both he and I were married. I justified it by believing that I was not cheating on her because it was not with another woman. There were times when I felt guilty, especially when I had to find a way to get away for a weekend with Tony. I don't like lying, and today I know the whole affair was wrong. I made mistakes, I'll be the first one to admit it. I'm not proud of what I did, but it's water under the bridge, and there is nothing I can do to change it now.

Although Tony said that he loved me, I didn't believe him. At one point I thought I loved him, but I think my relationship with him was more out of convenience. After telling him I planned to leave my wife, he asked me to move to Vancouver. He planned on staying here, however. He would not leave his wife because of his child. I told him I would not settle for being second fiddle any longer. He made me a lot of promises, offered me a lot of money, and said I would never have to work again. I looked at him and said, "No, I'm not living that way. I've lived that way for too many years. I've lied to myself and lied to everybody around me for too many years already."

Money was not what I needed. I needed the physical, the emotional being of that person with me. If I couldn't have that, I didn't want any of it. I didn't want a one, two, or three night-a-week stand. I would rather live by myself than live in a relationship like that. I ended my relationship with Tony in December 1985.

I also ended my marriage, which had already really ended. I moved out of the house in 1986. At one point I would say that I loved her, but I was never in love with her. I have had no contact with her for three years. We are not on good terms. When we divorced, I gave her the house, all the furnishings, everything. I signed everything over to her and walked away.

John, 61

Separating from my wife was difficult. I had many mixed feelings. I was very sad to leave the children but also felt that a huge burden had been lifted from my shoulders. Before separating, it had reached the point that every night when I came home from work, I would be subject to the same harangue about when was I leaving. It was also affecting the children. I was also afraid that I would be rejected by all of my straight friends and my partners. That simply didn't happen. I continued to be respected and cared for by most of my straight friends, both men and women. I did lose a few friends, but they were all people who had not been particularly close to me.

I bought my own house, and my wife and I began separation negotiations. It became an acrimonious relationship. We lost all contact with each other, but I had no problem continuing to have a good relationship with my children. I made a point of having them over at least once a week. They all did well in school and eventually graduated from university.

A few months after the separation, I was visited by a senior partner in the firm who told me I had a few options. He said that he had heard I was a homosexual, and I told him that he was correct. He said that he didn't know anything about it and asked to be informed. I remember saying to him that the gay world is the complete mirror image of straight society. There are many people who are gay who are decent, principled, disciplined, productive, loving, caring, creative people. There are also a number who are bums, and there are a mass of people in the middle. I said it's very much like the straight society.

This partner was interested, and he seemed nonjudgmental. He said to me, "Look, I'm here on behalf of a number of partners who need to make a decision on your future within the firm. My sense is that you probably don't have anything to worry about." I told him, "I intend to remain a hard working partner within the firm and maintain my involvement in the community as I have in the past. You will always find that I am a well-behaved partner." He left on good terms and told me that if I didn't hear anything in the next couple of weeks, I should just carry on. That was about twenty years ago.

I felt honored that they recognized me as a decent person and understood that I hadn't radically changed. He said to me, "You're the same person you were two years ago or five years ago." That was a very positive reinforcement for me.

On the advice of a friend, I went to see a counselor on the point of dealing with the children, as they would eventually ask a lot of questions. The psychologist said to me, "John, you should feel good about yourself and what you've done with your life." I received good vibes from the conversations I had with him. He said the only word of advice he would give me was never lie to your children and leave the door open for them. It turned out that none of the children ever came to me and asked me any questions. They pieced it together on their own.

David, 16

I came out to myself when I was thirteen. I don't know how I came to that point, but I guess I was having a hard time pushing down my feelings and attractions. It was really getting to me. I decided it might be okay to allow myself to be who I am and stop pretending to be someone I wasn't. I kept vacillating, though, until I eventually decided that I have to accept this. It's there and it's just going to make me feel worse if I keep denying it.

I don't think I ever had negative impressions, or stereotypes, of gay people to overcome. I was just afraid that if I was gay, it would be much harder for me because I thought people were going to hate me.

In actuality, a few of my friends have found out that I am gay and they're very positive about it.

I did wonder if being gay was morally wrong, however. What changed my view of that was meeting some gay people, and I also did more thinking about it. I had to accept who I was, like it or not.

One of my friends at school is a lesbian, and we do a lot of the same things together. She goes to the gay choir, I go to the choir. She goes to the gay youth group, I go to the youth group. I also wrote an article about gay youth that was recently published. I've become more comfortable being out in the community. Initially, I found it frightening to become more visible. Being out in community events has really shown me that it is wonderful to be gay. Something I've noticed about gay people is that they're generally warm and affectionate.

Last year at school there was a girl, Tina, who really wanted to be my girlfriend. As time went on, she increasingly wanted to become intimate. I was horrified. I've never felt sexual attraction to a female. I kept telling her that we would never become boyfriend and girlfriend, but it never sufficed. I decided that I would need to come out to her. I began by saying, "You know, I don't like girls as most boys do." She replied, "Well, I'll train you." I don't think she understood, so I finally whispered in her ear, "I'm gay." Her eyes popped out and then she stared at me for a minute, expressionless. She looked really uncomfortable and agitated for the rest of the day. She has never really accepted that I can't be her boyfriend. She still wants to cling to me even now. Whatever I do, I cannot get away from her.

I asked Tina specifically not to tell her parents yet, and she ended up telling her parents that evening. I don't want anyone else to know unless I tell them myself. Lately, however, I have been talking about gay topics at school. My friends respond well to these discussions. They're quite positive, and they think it's really interesting. Tina said to me the other day, "don't you think you're making yourself obvious?" I said, "Maybe I am, but if they find out, they find out." It will be a gradual thing. I think I want them to know. It's hard not being able to express yourself fully.

You asked me what it would be like to be out in either junior or senior high school today. I don't know for sure, but I think it definitely depends on what school you attend. In my school particularly, I don't know if I would feel completely comfortable, because our school is very ethnically diverse. Many students have grown up with religions that would not accept gay people. I still think it would be difficult.

I'm also one of few people with a physical disability in my school. If I ever come out at school, everybody will know it's not the purple walker that I've come out of. Remaining closeted at school is not easy either. I can sit at a school dance and think, "Gee, wouldn't it be nice to enjoy some slow dancing with that guy over there." I can't, however, because it's still considered unacceptable. I hate the unfairness of this. It makes me depressed. It makes me feel as if I am not allowed to express myself honestly to others.

I have a university friend who I was thinking of coming out to for a long time. I sat down, fully expecting that I might be totally rejected, or at least hear an, "Oh my God, you're gay!" I stammered and said, "Well, you know, I'm gay." He looked at me and said, "So? That's okay, that's fine." I thought, "That's it? Nothing more than 'so'?"

My lesbian friend is out at our school and although she admits that she hears the odd harassing comment, she shoots it right back at them. She is forthright and outgoing. I am more of a quiet person.

Recently, I have developed feelings for a guy named Greg whom I met at the youth group. A relationship would be impossible because of our age difference…he is twenty-two. By my standards it would be completely wrong. I don't think I would date anyone older than eighteen right now, and this poses a problem, as most people in my age bracket are not visible…they aren't out yet. Consequently, it's really hard to find someone my own age, particularly someone like Greg who also enjoys similar interests in the arts and drama.

Although I would like to be interested in somebody right now, my feelings toward Greg have caused me a lot of upset. For whatever reason, he is unable to even be a friend. If I call him, he doesn't return phone calls and things like that. He's a really nice person, but he's just not together enough.

I have often wished that the youth group I attend would advertise more. The same people always attend. Perhaps I'm looking for something that's too idealistic, but I don't think so. I think it's terrible that gay youth have a high suicide rate. I think that shows that there really isn't anything for us. If there were, I think there would be fewer suicides.

Glenn, 46

Before my 1984 trip to Britain, I admitted to myself that I was gay. I was alone in bed one night and I started crying. When I woke up the next morning, I said to myself, "Yes, I'm gay," but at first it seemed like nothing had really changed. The garbage hadn't been emptied, the bills hadn't been paid, the place looked like a mess, and the laundry hadn't been done. Before leaving my apartment that day, however, I looked at a sign taped on my door that said, "I'm great, God doesn't make junk." What had changed was that I now felt happy. I was beginning to overcome a major hurdle.

I later left for Britain with the objective of thinking about things and sorting myself out. I became very introspective on this trip. At two o'clock in the morning, while I was heading home to my hotel, an inebriated man opened his apartment window and yelled out, "Who gives a fucking shit?" Hearing that became a symbol to me. I realized that I didn't have to live up to someone else's expectations.

At ten o'clock in the morning, the maid began knocking on my door. I said, "I'm sorry, I stayed out late last night." I was tired and a half hour behind schedule. I have many rituals in London of things I like to do over and over again, and I was now late for my regular visit to Harrod's department store. By the time I made it to Chelsea, all hell was breaking loose. There were sirens and police cars and fire engines: complete and total pandemonium. As I proceeded up Sloane Street, I found out that an IRA bomb had exploded at Harrods a half-hour earlier. Six people died and about a hundred were injured. If I had been on schedule, I would have been near the store that sustained the most damage.

That incident made me start thinking that life is too short, and I decided to go out that night and get picked up. I knew I was about to have my first sexual experience because I was ready. It turned out to be wonderful.

Coincidentally, the fellow who picked me up was a member of the London leather community. He was into some bizarre sexual scenes and I tried to oblige him as best I could. I was reflective over the next couple of days and disturbed about what I had done, yet in a way it seemed natural to me. He was eighteen years my senior and a department head for a television studio. I had a role model of a mature man with a good job who was also gay. I continued to see him on subsequent trips back to London, and we became good friends.

I think through him is where I began to form a positive gay identity. I always think of him with a great deal of affection. Although he is rather a stereotypical, raving British queen, he is a genuinely warm and caring person. I think I was lucky to meet him.

Now I was out in England, while still maintaining a solitary life back in Calgary. I lived eleven lonely months a year here so I could spend my twelfth month free in England. During a trip in the mid-eighties, I decided that it would be my last. That decision was circumvented by my best heterosexual friend in London, Brian, asking me if I would be godfather to his youngest child. That was a great honour to me, so I returned to England two more times after that.

I continued to go to gay bars in London, and also to find my sexual expression in the leather bars. Throughout this time, I became increasingly involved in fetishes. I invested heavily in leather and latex clothing and the accompanying "toys."

At my high school's seventy-fifth anniversary, I ran into an old acquaintance who was now married. He classified himself as bisexual, and he was active in both the gay scene and the leather scene. I asked him if he would take me to a gay bar in Calgary.

He agreed and we went to two bars. I was dressed in leather and latex, and he wore full leather. We ended up going out every Saturday night for about three months. Gradually more people started showing up in leather. Seven months later, I became a founding member of one of the leather organizations.

Troy, 24

I started to detach myself from former friends and I spent the whole fall alone while exploring. I did research in the library and started reading everything about homosexuality. There was also a phone support line in Waterloo, and I remember calling it on weeknights. I wanted to know what was out there and what things were like. I was pretty hesitant.

I felt significant turmoil and fear. I believed that gay people are not normal; they're all freaks. The images in my head were terrible. For me, the worst stereotype was that all gays are effeminate. But then, just before Christmas 1994, I saw a poster for a "coming out" group that was being offered by a youth agency in Waterloo.

I started attending the group in January. That's where I first started meeting gay people. I was nervous at first, but I soon realized that these people were what I considered normal. It became a comfortable setting, and I ended up coming out that month. I immediately bonded with two guys there, and we became friends quickly. It felt so good to be with others and I started to go to the gay bars with them. I began to see the bars as a place where I could go and be safe. I could sit and talk with these people and flirt if I chose. I could be myself.

I developed my first physical relationship with one guy in the group. It lasted about two weeks. I wasn't attracted to him overwhelmingly, but I wanted to know what it was like. I trusted him and felt safe with him. I knew that this was what I wanted, and I didn't feel any guilt.

I went home for the summer and went to the gay pride weekend in Toronto. It was great to see the size of their gay community. Nearly everyone who lives around Church Street is gay. I felt really comfortable being there.

I came out to my mom that summer as well. Her reaction was great. She was like, "Hey, this is okay, don't worry." I was the one all shaken up. I was getting all emotional telling her, but it didn't change anything for her. She told me that she had suspected since I was a teenager. I was not yet ready to come out to my dad, however. Fortunately, I didn't feel any urgency, because my parents are not together. Both of them are remarried, in fact.

Following the summer, I went back for my last year at school, and I lived with a guy that I had met in the group. That was a really positive experience because I could be totally open and free and have someone to talk to about being gay. This guy was great. He had his head on his shoulders.

He introduced me to Warren in September 1995. It was amazing. We went to a movie the first time, then went back to his place afterwards, and I just freaked out. I was all nerves. Warren just turned on the television and made us some tea. I was expecting to be jumped or something, but I didn't know what to expect because I had never been in this situation before. I was attracted to him, but I was a wreck. I split fairly quickly that night, but the next weekend we went out and he told me to relax. He said we would take things slow and that he wasn't going to jump me.

Andrew, 29

During the school year, I worked at a straight bar in Montreal that was incredibly homophobic. It was owned by a man named Bruce and his wife, Janet. About a week after I started there, Bruce told the managers to fire me because he thought I was gay. They spoke with Janet, and an incredible fight ensued. Bruce eventually lost, and I kept my job.

Maybe two months later, Bruce watched me perform on an incredibly busy night. At the end of my shift, he looked at me directly in the eye and said, "I apologize, and I take back everything that I said about you." My performance helped him get over a barrier around my sexuality. I stayed there for the next four-and-a-half years. I also strategically dated waitresses there to maintain neutrality around my sexuality.

I had sex with these women, but this did not threaten my gay identity. I had complete identification with men as sexual and emotional partners. Having sex with women was physically enjoyable, but that didn't make me question being gay at all.

I attended McGill University between ages twenty-one and twenty-five, and I was twenty-two or twenty-three before I could say I was gay. I first disclosed to my sister and a close female friend, whom I knew would be okay with it.

I don't think it could have happened before then because there was too much going on. By that time as well, Karen had been reintroduced in our family, and Mom and Dad were doing a lot better with it. They accepted Karen and her partners, and she ended up moving back home. They even helped her get back in university. Today they enjoy an excellent relationship.

I had two boyfriends in Montreal, beginning at age twenty-three. My first boyfriend was a man named Jerry, but it was not anything significant. It was a process of discovery, as both of us were becoming active gay men while still dealing with our own internalized homophobia. The fact that we were closeted destroyed our relationship. It lasted five or six months.

Following this relationship, I was single again for quite a while before meeting Don. He had a really glamorous life. Although we never seemed to spend much time together, the time we did spend together was marvellous.

It took me about three months to figure out that he was married. I couldn't end the relationship then, however. I loved him. It lasted for about a year.

After our break-up, I found it difficult to function in Montreal because everything reminded me of him. I was pathetic and miserable. After applying to several law schools, I accepted an offer from the University of Alberta. I began there in September 1990.

I had a brief, two-week relationship with a guy who was a film set designer. He was in his late thirties and we'd go out for dinner. That was a new experience for me. I felt I could hold my ground on topics like Canadian and American politics, but when something came up around the history of HIV and AIDS, I knew absolutely nothing. I didn't know anything about Queer Nation, queer history, or gay culture. He looked completely aghast when he realized that I had no knowledge of gay history at all.

I thought, "How dare you be offended by me not having this depth around being gay." That was the beginning of my search for that information and history. I started reading, and it was shortly after that that I met Gary. We developed a healthy relationship that was honest and openly gay.

Alex, 23

As I was turning sixteen, I came out of the closet, fully and completely in my school, and dumped my girlfriend. Coming out to her was like an annunciation to the world.

My parents ended up moving to Toronto, and I moved in with them. Everything began to collapse. Things at home were just horrible, whereas the six months with my uncle were wonderful. I hated living back home, and school went downhill. I felt incredibly suicidal.

My suicidal feelings were not only the result of my parents. While I prostituted from ages twelve through fifteen, the first five times that I had anal sex were with men who forced it on me. I didn't know what to do about it. Was I supposed to tell my mother? "Mom, I was a prostitute and I was raped five times. Pass the potatoes, please." I wanted to die, and my father was driving me up the wall, too.

I was also bothered by thoughts like, "Oh my God, I'm gay. I can't live a normal life, I can't have children, I can't have kids." I also thought that nobody liked me and that school was horrible. I tried to play on the rugby team and I did really well, but Dad didn't care.

I was sixteen, and I wanted to die. I bought a gun and I had a hard time deciding whether I would use it on me or my dad. One night, while sitting beside a river, I began crying. I didn't know what to do. I had the gun with me, and I ended up throwing it in the river. I went home and packed.

The next day I wrote my parents a letter telling them how much I disliked living there. I moved out and never lived at home again. That was eight years ago.

I asked for help from child welfare in Ontario. They told me I wasn't eligible for services because I was sixteen. I told them that my parents were abusing me, but because Mom and Dad denied it, it took me sixty-two days to get services. I continued attending school while working part-time at a health-food store and prostituting every day. I eventually got my own apartment. Everyone in school knew I was gay. Then I meet this guy named Franklin.

Franklin was a gorgeous twenty-six-year-old model who also owned a clothing business in Toronto. We went to his place and showered before having sex. We started seeing each other regularly.

Franklin owned an expensive men's clothing store in Toronto. His partner, whom he'd lived with for seven years, was the fashion designer. I dropped out of school and began spending nearly all of my time with Franklin. I met everyone who was everyone in the gay community because they all came to his store.

Our relationship hit a peak during the summer. One day I woke up at Franklin's house with a really sore neck. I had a lump, and it hurt to move. The lump grew, and I began thinking I must be dying of AIDS.

I returned to school that fall. One day in class, I had to leave early because I thought my head was going to explode. I walked to my mother's doctor, who then rushed me to the hospital. The lump turned out to be an abscess. I called Franklin, and he arranged a private room for me. All of Franklin's friends, who I had already met, heard that I was in the hospital. My entire room became filled with expensive bouquets of flowers. I also had a $400 statuette with flowers around it that said, "I hope that you're feeling better." My parents were in complete awe when they arrived. They asked where all of this came from, and I told them about Franklin.

After my parents met Franklin, my mom asked if he was gay. I told her he was and that I was thinking of moving in with him. The day of Armageddon had arrived. She said if I did that, I should never call her. After I left the hospital, I stayed with Franklin to recuperate.

Franklin called my parents to tell them I was staying with him. They freaked out. I went home to talk to them, and after some fighting, I just said, "Mom and Dad, I'm gay." They said they knew. My father said, "It's all right, son, we'll bring you to a doctor." My mom, on the other hand, asked my older brother to kick me out of the house because I was gay. She told me to never come back and never call again. I said fine.

Chapter Six
Coming Out Summary of Themes

The Experience of Gay Men

Some of us began acknowledging that we were gay after experiencing some type of turning point or crisis. The intensity varied, but it could lead otherwise sane individuals to consider suicide seriously. Most of us experienced intense, negative emotions during our self-identification process. Guilt, anxiety, anger, embarrassment, and depression were common. Such emotions could drive us to despair. Fortunately, nearly everyone experienced another cluster of emotions. Along with the agony came a newfound joy. Ironically, the feeling of relief, exhilaration, and euphoria could seem overwhelming. We were not suffering from a mental illness like once believed in the past—instead, we were reclaiming ourselves.

This was not an easy task. The hindrances kept reminding us of the demon homophobia and it kept haunting us in many forms. It created doubt, and doubt could summon forth the defense of denial in an instant. We were already experts at its use. While our emotions danced in circles, our inner beliefs were metamorphosing. Reducing internalized homophobia meant correcting our own faulty stereotypes about gay people. Beyond these changes, many of us also needed to look deeper at what it meant to be gay. Our innermost beliefs, held dear to our hearts, had to evolve.

Approximately half of us needed to learn the gay role. Without having positive gay role models, we watched, we read, and we listened. We learned how to act sexually and nonsexually with other gay men.

The little bird who cracks open its shell cannot reenter it. We cannot go back either. When enough progress has been made in (1) accepting the gay label; (2) learning the gay role; (3) working through the emotions; (4) reducing internalized homophobia; and (5) becoming certain, the next evolutionary step becomes possible. Not all gay men seem able to go there, however. It speaks multitudes about the difficulty of truly breaking free of homophobia.

Discussion Regarding These Experiences

Labeling oneself as gay (i.e., self-identification) is an important transition into developing a gay identity. Many experience this as a turning point or a crisis (e.g., Paul's story). It is the time at which the fulcrum shifts from the side of the hindrances (e.g., the fear and condemnation of homosexuals), which has kept the gay man in the closet, to the side of the catalysts (e.g., the developing awareness of being gay and gay culture), which liberates him. Before this point, the hindrances and catalysts have battled, generally for years. Self-identification begins the challenging task of developing a gay identity.

The turning point for John was falling in love with another man. Quoting John from the "Before Coming Out" section of this book, "This relationship was the catalyst that helped me to come out to myself. I let myself be really what I am." Love became the impetus he could not deny.

One of the earliest gay theorists remarked that most people will need to change the meaning of the term *homosexual* before they can place themselves into that category.[38] This involves reducing internalized homophobia by breaking down the stereotypes and resolving other inner conflicts about being gay.[39] Much of this work occurs during the coming out phase.

There is an outpouring of emotions when gay people come out to themselves. These include both positive feelings and negative emotions. The negative emotions derive from two challenges: first, from the inner turbulence caused by coming out (and the process leading up to it), and second, from the external consequences that occur. We see a glimpse of the inner turmoil that Jonathan felt when he described his guilt about loving a man, having gay sex, and rejecting certain Chinese cultural values. Guilt is a common emotion with people who have not developed positive gay identities. Other common negative emotions include disillusionment; self-hatred and despise; fear and anxiety; sorrow, sadness, and unhappiness; loneliness; and ambivalence.

External consequences can also produce negative emotions. Pursuing happiness has been an important life goal for Jonathan, yet early in his coming out, happiness was thwarted. He initially felt undesirable by the sea of Caucasian patrons at the bar, which in turn cast doubt on his self-esteem. An older man later raped him, resulting in a number of negative emotions. Jonathan felt depressed after being in a sexual threesome, feeling that the third person only desired his best friend.

Now for the positive emotions: Tommy "didn't feel good having homoerotic attractions as a teenager," for example, but this had changed so dramatically by second-year university that he felt enthusiastic about telling people he was gay. Other co-researchers described feeling joy, exhilaration, and euphoria soon after coming out.

In essence, long pent-up feelings finally express themselves. These deep emotions have been submerged in a sea of denial and minimization, often for years, and now the pressure is explosive. The first time gay males experience sexual excitement toward another male, and feel good about it, the submerged emotions surge to the surface. At last, one is on the path toward wholeness.

Another aspect of coming out is learning what it means to be gay, and part of this involves learning new roles. Trying out new roles is a common aspect of identity development,[40] and gay people experiment with roles until they discover what fits for them.

These roles can be divided into sexual and nonsexual ones. The nonsexual roles include deciding which gender roles to keep or alter, and learning new ways to relate to other gay men. The gay community has greater tolerance and openness toward gender roles; toward many behaviors, in fact. Whereas gender roles are more clearly defined for heterosexual men, gay men have greater latitude. The gay community has not established rigid rules of either dress or conduct that everyone must follow.

Another example of assimilating new roles is learning to become comfortable in social situations with other gay men. As the gay community is diverse and the norms are relatively inclusive, one meets people from all walks of life with varied belief systems. Contrasted with the participants at heterosexual social gatherings, the attendees at gay socials are, relatively speaking, more heterogeneous. Their lifestyles, beliefs, and socioeconomic statuses are often varied. The thread that binds gay men together is sexual orientation and society's reaction to it. Apart from this, gay men are as different from each other as heterosexual men.

There is also significant diversity in the ways that gay men construct intimate relationships. Some couples are together for nonsexual companionship, others have open versus closed relationships, and others maintain casual relationships with a few men. Relating to such an array of differences requires learning and expansion of one's perspective. Consequently, gay men often have the opportunity to become more tolerant and accepting of others within the community.

Regarding the sexual gay role, learning to become sexual with another man is, at first, emotionally challenging for many gay men. Our society's taboo about intimate touch between men is at once confronted as internalized homophobia surges to remind gay men of it. This fear usually diminishes as sexual experiences with the same gender feels natural and right. Sometimes it is one's love for the other that sparks this awareness. There is still an awkwardness in learning to act sexually with a man and lucky are those who find a good teacher. Those are classes gay men will not want to skip.

There are often times when individuals question their commitment to gay identity, particularly soon after self-identifying as gay. Those who are still uncertain often say things like, "I might fall in love with a woman someday," or "If I work at it, maybe I can get turned around."

Indeed, many people exploring their sexuality may prematurely give themselves the label gay. The hallmark of being gay is about having the propensity to mostly, if not exclusively, fall romantically in love with members of the same gender.[41] This can take time to assess adequately. Just as homosexually inclined individuals are physically capable of having sexual relations with members of the opposite gender, heterosexual individuals are similarly capable of having sex with the same gender. Examples of the latter include individuals having same-sex relations in situations where the opposite gender is unavailable (e.g., in prisons) and between some individuals who have sexually-liberated, nonhomophobic attitudes. In such instances, the sexual act is usually merely an act, devoid of genuine passion.[42]

Most people need time to become certain of their sexuality. Becoming certain is an important step in developing a positive gay identity, and research supports it as leading to better psychological health.[43] It seems doubtful that most gay men would go on to develop positive gay identities if they remained uncertain about their sexual orientation. The momentum and courage that it takes to get beyond coming out begins from a place of knowing.

Without question, coming out is a challenging process. Before developing a positive gay identity, as I wrote earlier, positive feelings are juxtaposed with negative ones. The emotional highs and lows are occasionally extreme, and often frustrating, perplexing, disappointing, and exhausting. For those who develop positive gay identities, the high tide eventually subsides and the calm after the storm prevails. A gay male needs to ride these waves to get beyond them. They represent fragments of identity that are struggling to integrate.

Chapter Seven
Beyond Coming Out Stories

You are queer, you lucky fool, and that makes you one of life's buccaneers, free from clutter of two thousand years of Judeo-Christian sermonizing. Stop feeling sorry for yourself and start hoisting your sails. You haven't a moment to lose.

(Maupin, p. 93)

Matthew, 32

After reading your question of how I came to adopt a positive gay identity, I considered that there may be two sides to it. I think one side is that I identify being a positive gay person with being a positive person in general. That has helped me out a lot. Any issue can be approached with either a positive mind set or a negative mind set. My parents, especially my dad, often ensured that they approached things positively. They instilled that in me from the beginning.

I directed a theatrical show containing a gay theme in 1991. This was held in a larger city, and meeting a guy became my catalyst to move there. That's when things really changed for me. My sister and brother-in-law invited me to move in with them, but before doing so, I came out to them in a letter. I didn't want to hide anymore; that was one of my reasons for moving. I was tired of double talk. Both of them seemed okay with it, and I stayed with them for four months.

Then I lived with another gay person who I had met at work. For the first time, my circle of friends was largely gay. That was significant because then we could all talk about being gay, and it was okay, it was normal. I worked for a retail outlet that was filled with gay men, and I was completely out at work. At that point I would no longer accept any stereotypes or discrimination. I thought, this is who I am, and I'm allowed to be who I am. One of the first things I told people I met was that I was gay. I talked gay. I went out to the club and people were starting to find me attractive, which increased my self-confidence. I think people probably found me attractive back in university as well, but maybe I didn't allow them to get close to me.

I also had less to lose in this new city. I felt freer to do whatever I wanted. I could explore whatever, and my focus had shifted from theater. A lot of my self-image, I think, has come through my friends. It has affected me greatly to be around really positive, fun people.

I met two gay friends and started working with a group which was sending an athletic team to the next Olympic gay games. For the first time, I had an ongoing emotional attachment to men. I was initially attracted to them physically, but it turned into friendship. That really helped me feel good about myself and about being gay. I also became involved with various organizations. The guys I met were really positive, fun and ambitious. They provided an emotional boost to me. Through it all, my gay identity became stronger. Now it is who I am and anyone who's close to me has to accept that. When I sense that someone doesn't like that about me, I will not get close to them.

Coming out to others is more important for me now than ever. I want people to know that fairly early. If they can't accept that then they can't accept me. I'm not going to waste my time on those relationships. I really view it as "If you can't deal with it, that's your problem, it's not my problem. If you have a problem, then fine, you deal with it. Go away and deal with it."

I have felt the most pride in being gay generally at quiet times. I remember one significant occasion when I was alone, cleaning and tidying up at my store. I reflected on being gay. I remember thinking that I can't imagine not being gay. The thought occurred to me that internalized homophobia is the ultimate form of self-hatred. Everyone's sexual orientation needs to be respected.

I've also felt particularly proud of being gay during gay pride days. You think "Yeah, I feel a real sense of community here and I feel good about this." I remember feeling that the first time I walked in the parade. I felt "This is cool, we're making an impact."

I remember visiting Vancouver in 1994. I was having coffee and thought about how much I watch my actions and my body language when I'm in a smaller, more conservative city. I felt so much freer in the gay community in Vancouver. I sat with my legs crossed in a way that might be considered effeminate. At first I thought, "Oh, I shouldn't cross my legs," and then I thought, "Who cares? No one cares here." And that was a sense of freedom. It's small things like that. Times when I've been able to walk hand-in-hand with a guy have been significant.

My view of Christianity as a whole has changed dramatically. I wouldn't consider myself to be a Christian any longer. I have radically different views, and they are still in progress. I don't believe in heaven and hell, and I don't know if I believe in a personified God either. I don't pray because I think prayer is just a form of meditation. I think prayer changes things only in the same way meditation does. You think about things and it affects the way you go through life.

I feel comfortable with where I am spiritually, and I feel comfortable in not knowing. I don't think that I ever will know, and I don't need to know. I think my spirituality is in what I can offer to other people that I meet and how I affect the people that I come across day-to-day. I can give them a positive energy or a negative energy. It seems to me those people who are really spiritual are those people who are really worried about what happens after this life. I'm not concerned with that. I doubt that anything negative happens after this life. Why would it? Why would things change? Everything that decomposes turns into something else that is also useful. It has no moral value, good or bad. Because of that I don't fear death at all. If death only means the end of existence, nothingness, why would I be afraid of nothing?

In my continuing growth as a gay person, I am currently looking at the role that pornography plays in my life, and whether it is a positive or a negative influence. I am questioning how it relates to my desire for the perfect male body and whether it is why I'm not with someone right now. Am I looking for an Adonis? The flip side of that is, should I feel bad because I want to be with someone who is wildly attractive? One of my goals is to develop a long-term partnership with someone. I think that will be really important for my gay identity, and for my identity…period.

One thing that still bothers me is that my family doesn't accept my homosexuality. I wonder how they will accept someone who eventually becomes my permanent lover or partner. My parents will have to adjust.

Another question I have is whether I owe something to the gay community. I feel a sense that I need to give back something. I think in some sense I need to share my self with others and my experiences with others, or just my support. I have a sense of that.

Peter, 40

For a while, I was elated that I was gay. I thought, I'm really different, but I'm in control over my behavior. Suddenly, everything became so easy. I was so tired of contorting reality to make it appear that I was straight when I was obviously doing gay behavior. Then I started to come out to people. In one book I read, the author wrote that when you start developing a positive gay identity, you will want to come out because you won't like the dishonesty anymore. That's exactly what happened. Nobody wanted me to come out. Nobody asked me to come out. But hadn't I lied for enough years?

I invited my parents over one afternoon and I left a copy of the *Advocate* [a gay publication] on the table. My father picked it up, looked at it, and threw it back. I said, "Oh, that's the *Advocate*. Are you wondering why I have a copy of that?" "Well, we weren't, we weren't," replied my father, knowing full well it's because I'm gay. I told them, "Yes, I am." And that was it. The first thing my mother said was, "Well, is Jane a lesbian?" And I said, "You'll have to ask her about that, I don't know." My parents were some of the first people to whom I disclosed.

What I became was militantly honest. To this day, I despise dishonesty in everything because I lied for so much of my life and it took such a great toll. If I have a positive gay image, it's because I have a real sense of honesty. I don't think it's a positive gay self-image at all, but rather a positive image of the truth.

I'm out to everybody. I don't care who knows when it comes up naturally. I don't force the subject. When I left the legislature, I gave a few parting shots at the government about the way they handle gay rights during a radio interview. Although our elected representatives are all good people, even the homophobic ones, they don't know any better. They always had a hard time reconciling me with homosexuals because I didn't fit the image that they had of this faceless group. I had a face and they liked me and yet I was homosexual. I began to see how everybody else went to great lengths to contort reality to suit their needs, which is what I had been doing for so many years.

I was so tired of all the contorting we do in life, every day. I was determined that I was going to call a spade a spade. And when I saw that people had a hard time dealing with that, I began to realize that it was their problem, not my problem. I didn't have to make it easy on people for them to handle my being gay. I used to think, "How can I tell this to people so they won't overreact?" But I began to realize that if I was doing that, I was playing into their game. I was taking ownership of their inability to deal with it.

I believe "gay" people are those who identify as gay. They prefer same-sex relationships on an emotional, spiritual, and/or physical basis. I believe that if you're gay, nothing you can say will make you less gay or moderately gay. A good analogy is the idea of being a bit pregnant. You are gay or you're not. Although I believe true bisexuals exist and it would be inaccurate for them to identify as gay, they rarely do so. I don't like black-and-white images, but if you finally identify yourself as "gay" then say you're gay.

I thought the world would end if I came out, but it didn't. There have been some very negative experiences with my life since coming out. In fact, everything that's happened to me from a romantic point of view has been negative. That hasn't dissuaded me, however. I do have odd doubts, thinking maybe I would have been better to play the game and be what people wanted me to be. Then I think about it for two minutes, and I say, "Nah, it's not worth going back to the dishonesty."

Since coming out, I have had two relationships end solely because my partners could not handle their gayness. My first relationship was with Richard. He wanted his girlfriend to make a good show in front of his family, and he wanted me to take care of his physical and emotional needs. I said no way. Soon after this confrontation, he reconciled with his girlfriend, they engaged the same day, and they married about a month later. I haven't heard from him since.

I'm still in a grieving period over my last relationship, but I'm not letting it take me down. I had known Frank for years before we became intimate emotionally and sexually. After many months together, he began going through the same thing Richard did. Frank wanted me to butch it up and play it absolutely straight so that we would appear to others as simply good buddies, though maybe an hour before we had been in bed making passionate love. This bothered me, the whole idea that I was not able to acknowledge the special place that he had in my life. Here I had spent an entire lifetime coming out of the closet, getting rid of the lies, and Frank was trying to push me back in. I'm not going to be anybody's dirty little secret.

Frank panicked because suddenly he realized he was in a monogamous gay relationship. He told me that I was expecting too much, which infuriated me. I am not expecting too much. To suggest that because we're gay we shouldn't expect the same fulfilment out of a relationship as straight people is ludicrous.

After leaving the legislature, I started the company I have right now, which is immensely successful and humane; that's the most basic tenet. This is another club for me, but one that's within my control, without the addiction issues and stuff. Everybody there is so accepting, and it's a great environment to work in. A gay identity, a positive gay identity, occurs as strongly in a heterosexual context as it does in a gay context. You don't have to go to a gay place to express your positive gayness.

If there's some reason for the gay issue to come up when dealing with a vendor, we make them aware that these are gay dollars. For example, we forced companies to change their policies regarding same-sex spousal benefits if they wanted our account. I've got so much surplus money now that I gave a few thousand dollars to a gay group out east to help push through the national equal rights bill. I have given tens of thousands of dollars to other pro-gay groups as well. This is where I realize my positive gay identity. The surplus money goes to gay causes. I could work hours and hours as a volunteer and not achieve the same level of accomplishment that I do now by being able to throw a few thousand bucks at some project that is near and dear to my heart. I'm now able to be a philanthropist in the gay community.

Although I did not have a positive gay role model, I feel touched that I have been one to a number of others. I have received a few letters from men thanking me for helping them to come out. Through my visibility, others have found it easier because they learned that they didn't have to fit the negative gay stereotypes. I feel so proud when somebody tells me I had a positive influence on them. One of my major beefs concerns the lack of role models for gay boys growing up or girls growing up. Straight boys have Arnold Schwarzenegger, Wayne Gretzky, Magic Johnson, whatever. All we had were negative, horrible stereotypes. If there were gay portrayals at all, they were sneaky, effeminate, stereotypical negative gays and they all affirmed the stereotypes of this guy that molested me when I was nine years old.

Currently, my biggest issue as a gay man is that I'm very lonely, and I'm concerned that I won't find someone as positive as me. My happiness is not at its highest, but am I depressed about it? No. Am I willing to back down on my positive gay identity? No. The three men I have had relationships with are gay, but none have come to terms with it. Can I really blame them? I didn't come out until I was thirty-two or thirty-three. They haven't hit that stage yet. I know that I will never settle for a poor relationship. I'm waiting for a committed, proud relationship with someone who is healthy, who is self-aware, and who has gotten rid of the self-loathing.

Perhaps these types of individuals are right around me, but I'll never know them. We can be invisible to each other. If he really is healthy and doesn't have any affectations or signals that suggest his sexual orientation, I am obliged to assume he is probably straight. Likewise, he is obliged without such signals to assume that I am straight. We may be perfect for each other, but we'll never know it because we live in a heterosexual-dominated world, and that's sad—the realization that they may be around and I'll never know it.

I really hope that I'm going to have a relationship. That's what keeps me going. It will be an affirmation of these things that I know in my heart to be true. Eventually you need to taste the pudding, the proof is in the pudding. That being said, though, I think a person with a positive gay identity can do so much right now because there are so many people without a positive gay identity. What I do is send virtually thousands of dollars to something I feel has done something worthwhile for gay people. I can't think of a more positive contribution to my community, or my humanity, than to put a face on gay people.

Frank, 38

As I mentioned earlier, my first relationship was with Brad. My next relationship was with John, and although I thought I loved him, I'm unsure. He was probably seventeen or eighteen when we started dating, and all my friends thought I was nuts. I liked his company and enjoyed the intimacy that we had. When it came to summer, he decided to find a job in Toronto. That was his exit. I heard back through the grapevine that he was actually on the streets. He was hooking, which was devastating to me. I couldn't understand how that could happen, because I thought that we had had a reasonably good relationship. After a couple of years, I found out that he became HIV positive through these endeavours in Toronto, and now he's dead. There's no opportunity for any reconciliation.

I met Rob a few months later. About a year after we started dating, I was offered a transfer out west. After working in Calgary for three months, I decided to invite Rob to join me. We were together for almost eight years before breaking up. It was a hard break-up because we both had strong feelings for one another, and we had co-ownership in a house and had accumulated all kinds of things together. It was stressful for both of us. Since then, we haven't been good at communicating with one another. There are still too many feelings on both sides.

We had many things in common. We also argued. I always felt that he was an outgoing, vivacious, interesting, funny type of guy. As for us as a couple, it was always Rob and Frank, not Frank and Rob, that type of thing. I felt that my identity was being subdued. I wasn't getting treated the way I felt I should be treated in a relationship that had been going on that long. I didn't feel equal at all.

My relationship with Rob was good for the most part. I was proud of the fact that we had had a long-term relationship and that we had built a nice house together. We had met a certain circle of friends and I felt that we were respected as a couple. I think many people looked up to us as role models. This is what other people aspired to get to—a loving, nurturing relationship.

In the bar world, the common perception is that there are no long-term relationships. My retort is you don't see the long-term relationships because people haven't got the foolishness to come to the bar when they're in one.

I have a penchant for young men, which is probably going to get me in trouble in the long run. My most recent relationship was with a twenty-year-old. We had some trust issues and we also had incompatibilities about how to spend our time together. He wanted to spend all of his time alone with me, whereas I wanted to include friends in some of our activities.

Currently, my most important quest as a gay man is to find a mate.

Hopefully, when I find that special person, I will be totally comfortable in that relationship. I'm hoping at that point that I won't give a damn about who knows. I want to be an advocate in some regard, promoting the fact that homosexuality is normal in the spectrum of human relations. I want people to look to me as somebody who's gay and who is a decent person.

It's so hard for me to separate a gay issue from a nongay issue. They're just issues for me. My relationships are gay relationship issues, and I've had some relationship problems in this past year or two. I do not like being alone, I want to be in a relationship. I want to find someone who I can love, who's going to love me back, who I can cherish and who I can be proud of and grow with and learn from.

I have volunteered for gay-related causes for several years. I have been involved in many gay social organizations as well. I'm comfortable in a gay environment because nobody is going to give me a hard time about being gay.

I would like to get to the point where I'm completely out at work. That would be a nice goal, a nice achievement. Right now, however, I hope to advance in my career and I just don't see the benefit of telling anybody I'm gay.

I sometimes think I would like to be a gay politician, somebody who was a joining agent for the gay and lesbian population across Canada and the world: to be an advocate and an ambassador, that type of thing. I often feel that we have political clout and we just don't use it. There is infighting between gays and lesbians, which strikes me as completely asinine. We have so much in common, and yet there's so much friction between our two groups.

I would say the largest part of my identity is the fact that I'm gay, but that is still not what makes me who I am. What makes me who I am is not the fact that I'm this or I do that or I enjoy this—it's that I haven't found something that I identify with more strongly than being gay. If somebody asked me what's the most important thing you want to tell me about yourself, I wouldn't tell them I'm a New Brunswicker and I wouldn't tell them I'm an accountant for an oil company. To try to define who I am first and foremost, you need to know that I'm a gay man. I don't know if that's right or wrong, but that's just the way it is with me.

When I was growing up, my family tried to instill what being a good human being is. I've taken that and added the fact that I am gay. To be a good person means being a positive person and means having a positive gay identity. It's not specific to being gay in and of itself. It's just being happy with your lot in life and helping others and just being a good person. If you're gay while you happen to be doing that, then you've got a positive gay identity.

Gavin, 32

I strongly believe that the reason I am successful today is because of my sexuality. Excelling became a security blanket, in that I believed it would help in my acceptance of being gay. I felt that if I was on top of the ladder financially and socially, people could not come back at me and say, "Well, you're no good because you're a faggot." Consequently, I think my sexuality really pushed me to excel. When I look back, I realize the reason that I worked so hard in my late twenties, made so much money, wore certain clothes, and purchased the cars I drove was based on my discomfort with my sexuality. I realized I was proud of being gay on the surface, but I had created a shelter to make sure that nothing would come crashing down around me because of my sexuality. Once I realized what steps I had made to hide or legitimize my sexuality, I became aware of how deeply it had affected me. That's when I started to become a positive gay man. Now anything could come crashing down, and if somebody said it's because I'm a fag, it would not faze me at all. It would never be the excuse.

Even until two years ago, I would have been really nervous to hold hands with somebody in the car at a stop light or something. Then I saw the movie *Priest*, and it strongly affected me. It made me really, really mad when I realized how much being gay had affected me over my life. I realized that I had been oppressed since childhood. That made me look around and try to figure out what other aspects of my life had been affected.

After the movie, I sat with a friend at a local bar. We talked with the bartender, who was an openly gay man, and with a hairdresser who had been out since he was seventeen. He was absolutely flamboyant, and everyone knew he was gay. We started talking about the upcoming gay pride march, and it was divulged that neither of them had come out to their families. Furthermore, they said that they would never be caught dead at a gay rally or march.

I was just furious because I realized that for as much as they think they are out and living gay lifestyles, they are actually in complete denial. The reason I reacted so harshly was that I was hearing them and seeing part of myself in what they were saying. That really hit home, so the next morning I went out to buy a pride flag sticker for my car, because I thought it was a way to send a signal to other people. I felt that it was really important to get the message out that we are everywhere. In Canada today, you've still got to try to continue to grow and continue to be partly different. You need to realize all the different effects that the straight community and the world have on you.

When I went to the gay games in Vancouver, the feeling of seeing twenty or thirty thousand gay men and lesbians in one room was indescribable. You come out a completely recharged person. There are sixteen-year-olds, eighty-year-olds, people in wheelchairs, and every single thing is going on in that room, and it's really, really powerful. Friends have recommended that I go and stay for a month or so in a huge gay culture—not the West End in Vancouver or even San Francisco, but somewhere where it's just completely open. Sydney, Australia is apparently the place. I've been told that until you get into a situation where everything is completely open, where it doesn't matter and everyone is so accepting, you can't see the oppression that you're experiencing.

I haven't had an all-encompassing experience of being in love yet. I made the decision a long time ago that if I'm single forever, that's okay. I'm not going to make an exception. If it's not going to be perfect or near perfect then I'm not interested. I have no intention of camping out with somebody for six months and pretending it's all glorious. I have a very specific taste. If somebody is not a hundred percent physically attractive then I'm not really that interested. They also have to have a hundred percent of the personal qualities I look for as well.

I still have a really hard time relating to the average person. I can be dancing with a guy in a gay bar and someone will come up to me and say, "Why do you straight people come here?" For some reason, I guess I don't look gay. I'm not good at communicating with people in a bar. I still don't understand the politics of it, and I don't think it's a place that I would meet somebody anyway.

Talking about positive gay identity, two years ago one of my goals was to accept the subgroups of the gay community. For example, bears, drag queens, and leather types. I wondered why we had to be associated with these groups. I realize now that the entire community needs to be embraced, and again that was a pride issue.

As for my growth as a gay person, I still want to experience more in the gay world, more in a psychological or mental way than a sexual way. My goal is to continue to discover within myself and within the gay community whatever can make my life happier or other people's lives happier or easier. I've always felt that I have been extraordinarily lucky in the way that I grew up. I had a much easier time dealing with things like sexuality and solving life issues than many gay men and lesbians.

My positive gay identity is integrally related to my background, my upbringing, the size of the community here, and the negative reaction to homosexuality on the large scale here. The homophobia creates amazing dysfunction in the community and I personally feel that part of my having a positive gay identity must be the continuing education of others, whether they are gay, lesbian, or straight.

Being gay is about freedom from everything—absolute freedom. Many early Canadian explorers were gay, and they were allowed to be explorers because they had the freedom to do it. They didn't have families, they didn't have kids, they could do absolutely whatever they wanted. There wasn't the urge to settle down, and there wasn't the urge to get into a standard relationship.

Jonathan, 30

Through my parent's divorce, my mom and I became closer. Mom really liked Joe, my first lover, but she thought he was too old for me. He was twenty years my senior. We settled down together as a gay couple, and I became aware that we could have a normal life. Before this I had no idea you could live a normal life as a gay person. In fact I had no clue what type of life I would be leading once I became a gay adult.

From age eighteen to twenty-one, I had a wonderful time. My first job paid twelve dollars an hour, and I cleared over a thousand dollars a month. I was happy. I had a good relationship, I had a good income, we lived in a nice apartment. Joe took good care of me. He let me grow the way I needed to grow. He didn't shape me or mould me, he didn't say, "You're too feminine, don't wear that," or "It's too flamboyant." In turn, I contributed to helping him see how being gay can be a positive experience. I had nothing but praise for him. I gave him nothing but support, and over the years he said, "You are probably the most inspirational person to me." To this day, I still see him, and we talk like we were just old friends.

The biggest stereotype I had to overcome was that all gay people were feminine. It wasn't difficult, however. I would pick up a gay magazine and notice gay cowboys and other butch-looking men with great chests, who would go to the bar without wearing shirts, and I couldn't wait to explore for myself!

The early 1980s were my favorite times because all the men were masculine and the music was great. Brad, who became my best friend, took me under his wing when I started going to the second gay bar I frequented in Calgary. I felt some sexual attraction for him initially, but that soon dissipated as we became close friends. He had a beautiful big chest from working out regularly, he was tall, he was a professional, and he was funny. I especially liked his connection with his male friends in the bar. Everybody knew him and he knew everybody. He was inspirational and he became my role model.

I would say I had developed a positive gay identity by age nineteen. In adopting a positive gay identity, the biggest journey for me was to try to find happiness with who I am. I realized I could be a professional, and I knew that I could have a gay lifestyle and be public. Before, I thought you had to hide, but I was wrong. Some of my best gay friends were these big butch guys that had really good jobs. I discovered that all gays weren't hairdressers or feminine types. I met bank managers, construction workers, and police officers, for example. I was amazed at the number of gays who were in professional jobs. The excellent relationships I have had were the ones where I attained a positive gay lifestyle with men who were not afraid to be gay.

When Joe and I broke up, I moved into a building right next to my mom so that I could be closer to her. In 1986, I bought her a house and we both moved in that summer. It was fantastic. It was difficult growing up in an Oriental family and realizing that because you are gay, you will not fulfill a lot of the obligations of an Oriental grandson. It took me a long time to value my gay identity and my Chinese identity equally. Before that, I valued my gay identity more because it was more important to be true to myself. Then I attributed being happy to being gay. I thought I could either choose the Chinese lifestyle, maintain my Chinese traditional values, and leave the gay lifestyle behind the scenes, or I could do the reverse. I used to think of these identities as separate before I could merge them together and begin valuing Chinese gayness. This took considerable thinking.

I tried to please my family with their values, but I was trying to lead a positive gay life as well, believing that I had to do this for myself. It finally dawned on me that I could have the best of both. I have successfully done that. I am showing my mother that I've got an education, I'm financially successful, I'm still the loving son, I support and take care of her, and I'm gay. My mom and I have a wonderful relationship, and she loves my present lover to death.

Today I still wonder whether I would have come out if I had stayed in Hong Kong. I learned Western ways about kids getting to do what they wanted. If I hadn't learned these types of personal freedoms, I don't think that I would have turned out the same way.

I feel that I am a complete gay man, and I am no longer in conflict about it. I have some personal issues that relate to not wanting to be alone. Sometimes I get concerned about growing old alone.

In my present job I have not come out to the people who could affect my chances of promotion, but I don't think I would be afraid if they did find out. I don't think it would affect my chances of career advancement.

What I would like to do now is give back to the community what I got out of it. I have tried to help some younger gays turn their lives around and develop a positive gay attitude and a good lifestyle. I've been successful in two or three cases.

There are studies that say that the average gay person doesn't earn more than minimum wage. I think your financial status certainly plays a role in how you develop a positive identity, whether you are gay or not. There is a gay impression that you have to wear the best clothes and always look good. Money certainly plays a role in this.

Some people have a really hard time enjoying gay sex. That has something to do with identity. I can't remember if I read it or if I talked to somebody about it, but I think there are many people that have an illusion about gay sex. Having a positive gay identity doesn't mean that you necessarily have good gay sex. I remember after getting raped, I didn't feel like that's all gay sex was. However, I think many people who are trying to decide if they are gay or not could be deeply affected by that type of negative experience. If you had a negative gay experience when you were still deciding, that could deter you from having a positive gay identity as you progress through your life. I'm not saying that having a good sex experience at the beginning will necessarily lead to a positive gay identity either, though, as it all depends on the other factors that come along with it.

If you really haven't admitted that you're gay and you go and have gay sex, guilt can drive you toward not having a positive mental attitude about it. Guilt played a big part in my life too. I think that would play a big part in other people's lives because of society's disapproval.

It was really hard to not feel guilty about wanting to love a man. I probably finally dealt with it when I was about eighteen. Brad and his friends helped me get over my guilt. I decided that I didn't have to feel guilty about going to the bar or holding another man in my arms, and I didn't have to worry about other people. In fact, I had one little incident when I was in San Francisco five years ago, while holding hands with another man in their gay ghetto. I had a hard time because I worried about what other people would think. I challenged myself with this fear, however, and it went away really quickly.

Another thing that affected me was the lack of knowledge about other people in society who are gay. I wouldn't call this a lack of gay role models, but simply that many gays are so invisible that you don't realize they exist everywhere. Nonetheless, I think role models are important to establishing a gay identity.

Even gay people make discriminations of other gay people. When I realized there was a butch crowd to hang around with, I became part of that group. I remember saying things like, "You know that guy is so nellie," or "Once you're a drag queen, you're always a drag queen"—that type of discrimination. It's only been in the last three years that I've gotten out of that habit, that shell. I think we need to develop our own role models by appreciating that we are all one community and we can't afford to discriminate against ourselves, because it certainly affects other people. If those who have these traits are being ridiculed by other gay people, it will be difficult for them to develop a positive gay identity. Furthermore, people observing those who discriminate may learn to ridicule other people, which causes yet further discrimination. If we are ridiculing ourselves, our own people in our community, what that says to society is that it is okay to ridicule us. That defeats our entire cause of trying to gain acceptance in society.

Gay means a lot of things. Saying that I accept being gay means I accept all the things that gay people are. If, when you accept the fact that you're gay, you then turn around and compare yourself to others, that's wrong, because being gay is not just about yourself. It's about everybody.

Jerome, 48

I became actively involved in several gay and lesbian organizations in town, and I started a number of them over the years. Becoming more involved in the gay community helped immensely, as the people I met gave me strength and the social connection that I needed. I started meeting a lot more gay men who were decent individuals and who lived their lives very reasonably. I began to see myself as a person who deserved respect as a gay man and who could function as a gay man.

Eventually everybody in the city knew I was gay but my family still didn't know. It's usually the other way around. I began by telling my siblings, and they all had different opinions about whether I should tell my parents or not. In the end, I decided I was going to tell them. I told my father first, and he didn't seem all that surprised. It wasn't a big deal to him, and in fact our relationship continued to get better as he and I got older.

My mother's first reaction was, "Oh, I don't think you should tell your father," and I said, "I already did." She replied, "What? He never told me?" Both my parents were well educated. My mother was a psychiatric nurse and I think she had a lot of understanding about being gay. Both read a great deal and stayed current with things. My mother is actually proud of me. My father died a few years after he knew and has been dead now for twelve years.

Because of being open and public, I have been subjected to a fair amount of discrimination and harassment. I believe I didn't get some higher promotions and some tasks that I would have if I wasn't gay, but this is impossible to prove. I've done many radio shows and call-ins, and people call and say all kinds of terrible things, like "You should be shot," and "Your kind is awful," and "We'll get you." I've had calls at home, and I've had letters sent to me with similar messages. I had my electricity turned off once because somebody found out where I lived. I've learned to live with it in terms of knowing what it is, knowing that it shouldn't happen, and knowing that society needs to change.

I remember at one time saying to call-ins that they have every right to their opinions. That changed after somebody said something really nasty to me. I replied that I don't believe that nonsense and you don't have the right to say that to me. The next time somebody called with obscenities and hateful words, I yelled right back at them on the radio. Now I don't take that. I have as much dignity as anyone else.

When you read hate mail, it's a different experience then when the crap is blasted in your ear. Reading "You fucking faggot, you should be shot," or "What have you had for breakfast?" is revolting. The frequency of these sorts of threats and hateful comments goes up and down. Since I've been elected, if we are dealing with something that relates to being gay or lesbian and I'm part of that or quoted, I sometimes get some calls or letters and then it drops off again.

I have also been gay bashed a couple of times in the past. I was grabbed and slugged around fifteen years ago by some fellows that had been drinking and were looking for a faggot to beat. In the second incident, I was again grabbed and slugged and had my watch stolen. I was in an area where the assailant was looking for someone gay to grab and assault. Thankfully, no incidents have occurred since I moved here.

My growth as a gay person is a lifelong journey. I think for my generation it's a never-ending process. I am continually dealing with overcoming my own internalized homophobia. For example, my compulsive working certainly stemmed from compensating for being gay.

Though I am openly gay and publicly gay, there are still times that I don't acknowledge it when I should, in public settings. I think I also have some fear of growing old and alone. I don't really believe it, but there is some of that there.

As for my own gay identity, publicly acknowledging that I'm gay was certainly a major breakthrough for putting the pieces together. Leading the different lives had become harder and trickier to do successfully and I resented having to do it. I needed to integrate my identity and I was ready for it. Sometimes you need a kick in the butt. That might not have been the best way to get a kick, but it worked.

By accident, I became heavily involved in dealing with AIDS from a social-political perspective. I became a co-founder of an AIDS organization, and I was their spokesperson for the first two years. The major newspaper named me citizen of the year for my work with AIDS.

Those kinds of things have reassured me that I can integrate all of my life as a gay man and make it work in a way that is productive for me personally and hopefully reasonable for the society I live in as well. I am inspired to make some changes in this world, and I am directly involved in helping to do this as a politician.

Fréderic, 38

I learned the importance of making friends who would accept me, not merely tolerate me or try to change me. What has really influenced my gay identity the most are my friends, and mostly my straight friends, in fact. Many of the friends I had were straight women. I suspect that if you look at the history of disclosing, you would find that gay men have had a better ear with women, as compared to men. I felt I was bringing up something to my straight friends that was positive and that was important to me. They had many questions for me, and that helped me to solidify my identity as a gay man.

I fell in love with a gay man while at CEJEP, but it became a sour relationship because I was only attracted to him physically. His spiritual side was not what I needed at the time. He was my first love, however. He came to visit me in Quebec City once, and my heart pounded. I wrote stories and poems about him, but I ended the relationship rather drastically about a year or two later. Some of my straight friends sat me down and said I was wasting my time with him. Although it had never been anything sexual, he was unfaithful to me and a few others he dated.

In 1982, a year before finishing my degree, I met John, an English-speaking guy from Alberta, who was doing graduate work in

Montreal. He knew how to speak French, and I was attracted to him. He was the person that would turn my life 180 degrees around about gay positiveness. John had a lover at the time, so we never dated, but he became one of my best gay friends.

I met another friend, Greg, the same year, and he has become one of my closest gay friends. Next to John, he became the second most influential person in my life. He now lives in Victoria. He has never given up on me, and I have never given up on him. John taught me the road, and Greg said I'm going to walk with you on that road. They became the brothers I always wanted. Neither were nosy. They experienced my life with curiosity and without a desire to infiltrate or change me. They really respected me.

When John moved back to Alberta in 1982, he asked me if I would move back with him for the summer and learn English. Although my family was unsupportive of my plan, I decided to do it. I found a job in a summer camp and I started to learn English. John saw in me the power to learn something new, and he really helped me to realize that I would become who I wanted to be.

The summer I moved to Alberta, I had the time of my life, and this is when I realized that Calgary would become a cornerstone in my life. The next summer I worked again at a summer camp. I began to realize that I had something special for kids, and I decided that I would work with kids for a long time. When I returned to Montreal, I finished my degree. I thought I wanted to do a masters degree in history, so I moved back to Quebec City to spend a year with my mom. Everything was positive with my mom. We never talked about my gayness, but I am her youngest son, and there is a special relationship between us, especially since Dad passed away.

My year there, however, is when I suffered my first depression. This is when my past sexual abuse began to churn within me. I returned to Montreal and went for therapy to deal with the incest. During the therapy, I became confused about my sexual orientation, and doubts about whether I was gay or not emerged. I needed to learn to become comfortable with who I was sexually, and eventually it happened. The therapy helped me regain confidence in myself, and after that I registered at the University of Calgary to take a degree in education.

In 1987, I wrote a letter to my eldest brother, confronting him with the abuse. He replied that I had a chip on my shoulder and he didn't recall any of it. This autumn he wanted to come here and visit me, but I told him I wasn't interested in having him. I told him I didn't want him around me. The last stage is the one where I will confront him one day and tell him exactly what my heart feels. That's the stage where I will forgive him, but I can't do that right now.

There is a great deal of disenchantment in my family because I told some of my brothers about the incest, approximately two years ago. Right now, I have a poor relationship with my gay brothers, but a good or excellent relationship with my straight brothers.

As I discovered my sexuality from 1985 through 1988, I gradually gained control of ejaculation. Ben was one of my first lovers, and with him I was sexual and loving it. I was also more open about my feelings sexually. Ben was a man that I deeply loved, and the physical aspect was excellent. Ben confirmed in me that inside the bed and outside the bed could be great, but he had another lover that he would see occasionally. After a while, I couldn't deal with sharing him with somebody else. I drew a picture for him that had several doors in front of me, and it symbolized the choice I had to make about being gay and wanting to learn about it.

I was not surprised, and in fact somewhat glib, when one of my friends, Luke, told me that he was HIV positive. Luke sent me a message that I should get tested. He died in 1988. Another close friend who lived two blocks away from me died the same year. This was my first visual encounter with AIDS, and that was frightening. I was trying to decide if I would get tested or not, and suddenly people all around me were dying of AIDS. It had a major effect on me. It didn't take long for me to realize that what was in my friend's backyard was now in my backyard.

I felt somewhat of a dilemma between 1987 and 1990, before I got tested. In 1990, maturity became a vulture in my life. As it flew above me, it gave me an artist's view of a reality I had not faced. I had played ping-pong with my doctor: was I going to get tested or not? I used to panic and cry when I heard that some men that I had had sexual encounters with were infected with HIV.

I got tested, and the result was positive. I sat down and felt that everything had collapsed on me. However, my world didn't collapse. Instead, I entered a new coming out process.

Each decade had its new process of coming out. I first came out as a gay man, and it helped prepare me for this second coming out as a person with HIV. For example, I don't think I would have dealt with it in 1986. I think I would have killed myself.

I am now two kinds of gay positive. I am the positive gay and HIV positive. So there we go! Unfortunately, from 1985 until 1990 is possibly when I would have infected the most people with HIV. That is a very sad thought for me.

I told you earlier about my first lover, Ben. Just before he died from AIDS, he told me he was sorry that he poisoned my life. I told him that he didn't know he was infected when he was with me. We had had unsafe sex, but I had also had other sexual partners. I told Ben that I could not pinpoint who had infected me with the virus. Anyway, it was important for him to say that to me. Likewise, it was important for me to tell him that he had enriched my life and I'm glad for that.

It took me years to tell my friends. I think that with HIV the coming out is more the coming in: you have to do some inside cleaning first. You have to work through the anxiety by searching inside yourself before you can tell anyone else. You have to go through guilt, you have to go through losing friends to AIDS. You panic for yourself, you panic for others, they die, and you react, "Oh my God, I will too." It was nine months before I told one close friend. One friend told me to never cry about that. She helped me believe that I could deal with it. One of my strengths is that I am a positive person. I love life. That's an important aspect of who I am.

I didn't have sex from when I received my results until 1994. My decision was based on fear. It's not easy telling people who are potential sexual encounters that I am HIV positive. My HIV isn't going to run and hide in a closet. It will be with me for the rest of my life. At times I have felt hopeless.

In 1992 I decided to attend an AIDS organization so I could belong to a group of others who are HIV positive. I began integrating more positive thoughts about being HIV positive, and I started telling more people too. Then I met somebody with whom I started having a relationship. He was also HIV positive, but his health was not good. This was such a profound event for me, because I really fell for him and I really had a good time with him. It was also difficult because he felt incapable of building a long-term relationship. Our relationship lasted a summer. I wanted to date somebody again after this experience, and I started to have some sexual encounters again.

Telling my friends became another positive bridge. Although being HIV positive was a sad revelation, it turned out to be another wonderful event. When you tell somebody that you are HIV positive, there is an outpouring of very deep feelings. When I finally told my closest brother, he told me how much he loved me. The revelation creates a deadline to your life and your relationships. The HIV virus has taught me the importance of friendship as a gay man. It reinforced for me the importance of cherishing the moment. This has also taught me to respect life because each person that departs this earth has left me with something.

I have chosen not to tell my two gay brothers that I am HIV positive. One major reason I wouldn't tell my eldest brother is that he is a gay moralist. He has a Reagan vision of AIDS: "You deserve it. You were looking for it. Good for you." I wrote down my will this summer and really outlined that this brother cannot be at my bedside when I die. I might change my mind if something happens between him and me, but not right now. I think that a part of me also feels a certain guilt.

Nobody knows at school that I'm gay or HIV positive. Some of them know or suspect strongly that I'm gay, but I have never told them. My HIV status hasn't been disclosed at all, although I am thinking seriously about it right now. When I become ill, I don't want it to create a big collapse, downfall, or crisis. I need pillars at school, too, because I need friends to help me go through this.

I want to draw three close friends who have died of AIDS in the sky. Three of them holding hands with a ribbon in the middle, the earth in front of them. The ribbon will have written on it something like, "Please help me to go through this." That's my spiritual bond. What I do in my art, I do in my teaching and in my approach to life.

My gay identity has been challenged by being HIV positive from the perspective that AIDS is still a closeted thing. Why is it closeted? The more educated you get, the more you learn to not do this and not do that. The dilemma with being HIV is if you don't have a partner or if you're not in a monogamous relationship, you will need to meet people to have sex with them. You have to work on saying to yourself, "I am HIV, but this doesn't mean I am a second-class citizen." You are not a bad person because you are HIV positive. There are many gay men who have had more sexual partners than you, and they remain HIV negative. Some of my friends told me, "Fréderic, you got infected, and I still wonder why I didn't get infected." You have to stop making self-accusations. I have a sense that maybe a part of me has done something wrong, however. I haven't been able to totally cleanse myself of that feeling.

When you tell potential lovers that you are HIV positive and they run, I would like to say to them, "My name is Fréderic, my name is *not* HIV." You can see Fréderic and HIV, and I will be fine with it, or you can see Fréderic alone and I'm fine with it, but if you see HIV and you don't see Fréderic, I can't deal with that. I am thirty-seven and I've spent thirty years of my life not knowing I was HIV positive and only seven knowing I am HIV positive.

I believe that having other individuals around me who are HIV positive, gay or not, and having to tell friends has helped me become a positive gay man and a man who has a positive attitude about being HIV positive. I have found a tremendous power through my friends. I have also discovered another power: my family. The three brothers I told, and their wives, are highly supportive.

When you have a terminal illness, you need to do what I call "house cleaning." You will need to deal with unresolved issues if you want to have a better ending to your life, and you also need to deal with the life you have remaining. To date, I have not had any major illnesses related to HIV, but I have experienced a few minor symptoms. I have felt fatigue occasionally. I made a decision this year to slow down. I did too much and I paid a price.

I am sensitive these days about being with families. I need one thing right now: children. I think the child in me and the child that expresses itself is wonderful. The children I teach have often told me, "Boy, you're crazy," and that's because they see that I don't judge. When I go to a family, I really want the kids to know that I am gay. A balanced family was missing in my life, and I want children to know in a family setting that I am another member of this society and it feels good.

One of my goals is to experience family as a gay positive person. My sense is that my own blood family isn't here. I don't intend to move back to Quebec, but there is a longing. As a gay man, belonging is not everything to me, but it still means a lot. We grow and we participate together. As we go through thick and thin, remember that these two highways are not side-by-side—they eventually link.

My philosophy of life rests on one very important theme: it's not what happens to you that matters, but what you do with it. Upon reflection, I had the happiest childhood anybody could have until age ten. It became more confusing between fourteen and twenty. My twenties were about recapturing a sense of my life, and my thirties have been about learning a new aspect to integrate into my life.

Tommy, 41

I came out to my parents because I wanted to be closer to them. It was disastrous. I wrote them a letter and told them I was gay. Subsequently, I received long letters from my dad telling me it was a sin and that it was horrible, and how could I disappoint my mother and my grandfather and all these people. It's sick, you should get counseling, and so on.

I figured if they didn't understand this, then there was just no sense in continuing a relationship. I didn't go home for over five years, and I didn't write them, although my mother kept writing. At some point I just said, "Well, that's their attitude and they're still my parents" and I started going home again. We just didn't talk about my being gay. Before my dad died, he went out of his way to let me know that he accepted the fact that I was gay. It was a slow process. My mother and I still don't talk about it.

I didn't anticipate it would be this difficult for them to accept my gayness, but even if I had known this beforehand, I would still have told them. I was willing to give up everything because I accepted myself. It was my liberation. It was like a religious experience, finally feeling whole and not hiding anymore. I wasn't going to play games with my parents. I told them because I wanted to become closer to them.

Regarding spirituality, I rejected the teachings of the Catholic church quite quickly and easily. I realized it was an agent of social control, so I felt no remorse or loss in spurning it. I'm more collective in terms of my religious beliefs, and I think if you read the Bible, the emphasis is on community and friendship, with little focus, actually, on sexuality. The sexuality in religion was imposed by the Catholic church.

By 1981, I was no longer involved with the gay club. I developed a relationship with Carrie, which lasted for a year and a half. We were good friends and she knew I was gay, but out of personal intimacy we developed a sexual relationship. Our sex life was satisfying, but I would compare it to sleeping with a man you don't find attractive sexually.

Eventually, she wanted more than I was prepared to give. I lacked motivation to become more committed to her. When I started dating other guys and having relationships with them, it became more difficult for her to accept me as a friend. She still wanted to have sex, but I wasn't interested. I was seeking out male relationships, not female relationships. It doesn't mean I didn't love her, however. I felt very close to her. We continued to be fairly good friends for a long time while we both dated other boyfriends.

I was fairly independent in that I didn't like volunteering within the established gay community organizations. Instead, I started my own gay tabloid in 1984. Only three issues were published, but it was over a full year. I was very positive then, very action oriented, and I loved it. We had a gay march one day, and a picture of it appeared in our paper. It was very extroverted, very out. We were doing it for the community, and I think I was quite radical. I wanted to change people's attitude about being gay. I felt that the city then was pretty negative. The gay bars were the biggest element in the community and unfortunately, that continues even today.

At that point my gay relationships didn't really seem to take any particular direction. I had gone through a very public time of being gay, and after stopping production of the magazine, I dropped out of the gay community almost completely. I never went to gay dances, I never went to any organizational meetings. I think I had saturated myself with being gay. In my early thirties, I stopped having sexual relationships. Partly it was fear of AIDS, and partly it was my own attitude. My gay life had stopped, and this continued for eight or nine years.

When I started having sex again, it was tremendous. Three years ago, I met Robert, and although our relationship only lasted three months, it was significant to me. After Robert, I had a couple of tenuous sexual flirtations and then I dated Brent for a year. It was a nonconventional relationship: enjoyable, but limiting. I realized that it wasn't really going anywhere and it soon ended. I now wanted a committed relationship.

I now accept the fact that I can have relationships with people and it doesn't have to be a terrifying event if it ends. I think that is part of my identity now. I don't think I have to define myself in terms of a relationship, either. I would like to have an intimate friendship that could maybe evolve into a relationship, but I don't need it.

I don't think I have had many really positive gay people in my life. I've become more cognizant of the negative influences in my life. I am trying to associate with more positive individuals. For example, Brent never drank at all. At that level, I feel that was a positive relationship. I've discovered that it is possible to have a better quality relationship now as an older gay person than I did when I was younger. I am more accepting of myself and more accepting of other people. I'm optimistic that I will find another relationship, but it will take some time. Establishing a positive gay relationship has not been an easy task for me. This is my challenge.

Another challenge in developing a positive gay identity is learning how to survive in a straight world as a gay person without compromising your values. The world in which we live is predominantly heterosexual and it supports that lifestyle. You really have to look deeper if you want to find things that are gay positive.

To continue developing a positive gay identity, I would like to pursue activities that will help me meet another male for a long-term relationship. I want to be open to it. I'm also thinking about aging and where I will be in ten, twenty, and thirty years. Now that I'm in my forties, those issues have become more important. My gay identity will influence the direction I go in the future with respect to decisions I make about long-term lifestyle.

An issue I still need to resolve for myself concerns codependents and alcoholism in the gay community. I once chose friendships with people who were abusing drugs and alcohol. Sometimes I wonder why, and my best answer is that I surrounded myself with people who wouldn't challenge me. I changed that attitude at some point. I went through a period of rejecting people who were alcoholic, and I'm still very conscious of that when I meet people. If they abuse substances, I don't want to associate with them. I now chose friends who are non-substance abusers.

From an identity point of view, struggling with alcoholism, codependency, and drug abuse were definitely themes in my life. I used to smoke a lot of grass. Was there a fundamental flaw in my self-acceptance? Did it tie in to the fact that I was gay? Was it rooted in other elements of my personality? It's not easy to put my finger on these things. I think when I came out I had a very positive identity. These other issues became more important in my life than my gay identity.

In the 1990s, I have wondered about the influence of pornography in my life. I was highly addicted to it for several years. It became a mental exercise to have an orgasm without also consuming pornography. It took a lot of effort to get it out of my life. I wasn't sure I could do it, but I've done it. I think an addiction is when it prevents you from doing something else that you would place value on. I think my addiction to pornography kept me from pursuing intimate relationships.

I still meet people today who can't come out to their families for a multitude of reasons and they end up living a double life. Some get married, some are my age and some are younger. There are kids in their twenties who are still getting married to appear straight and yet they know they are really gay. This boggles my mind. I understand that it's their personal choice, but I don't think it's particularly positive. I think being gay infers being honest with yourself.

Cliff, 30

I came out to my mom five or six years ago. She already knew I was gay. She had found my gay pornographic magazines when I was twelve or thirteen. I went over to her place and showed her a bunch of drag videos: shows from the bar and some from the Fringe Festival in Edmonton. After watching the videos she said, "Well, you're pretty, you look like you have fun, and you're good at it, as long as you're happy." Finding out that I did drag wasn't much of a shock to her, as she had already seen drag queens before. Her main concern was that I wouldn't contract the HIV virus.

My dad does not or chooses not to understand anything about my gayness. There is no room in his life for gays. I may be putting words in his mouth, because he has never said anything to me, but he won't accept me. Rather than bring it up, he won't even talk to me.

The last big episode with my dad occurred at a family reunion. I had no interest in going, because I consider my family to be here: my gay family, that is. My friends are my family. They are the ones that make me feel loved. There are several friendly people in my family of origin and I like many of them, but there isn't love there. I'm the token gay relative, and I won't be that.

I told mom I wouldn't be at the reunion, so that Dad would go. He went, and he was really crabby. My cousin fought with him at the reunion. He defended me to Dad by explaining that I wasn't any less of a person just because I'm gay. At Christmas, another cousin got in on Dad and told him that if he wasn't such a prick, I would have been there too. He just refuses to deal with it. He won't accept that he has a gay son.

His birthday is on Christmas Eve, so usually Mom will phone me or I'll phone her. She tells me to wish my dad a happy birthday, and I'll go, "Merry Christmas, happy birthday!" and he'll go, "Yeah," before giving the phone back to Mom. Last year I was the only sibling to phone him on his birthday, and yet I'm the only one he doesn't talk to. There's no connection between us, and we have nothing in common. We haven't had any real communication for thirteen years. I wish he loved me, but he doesn't.

Conversation with my entire family is difficult. They are a dysfunctional family. My sister was spoiled because she was the baby and she was the girl. Today we get along very well. My brother and I were always at odds with each other. We would run around the house screaming and yelling, throwing knives at each other, and slamming the door.

He smashed the cars and trucks that Dad bought him, and he racked up driving charges—yet in my dad's mind, I was the bad one? I haven't seen my brother for about six years. We live different lives, and we have nothing in common. He's straight, married, has a baby, and is now getting a divorce. He has also become a cokehead.

In Regina is where I first did drag. It wasn't good drag, however. I didn't wear eye shadow or eyelashes. My friend and I were hanging around a lesbian, and we went through her closet one day. We decided to dress up, go to the bar, and see whether we would be noticed. We got a lot of attention, so we did it for a couple weeks. By this time I wanted to move back to Alberta, and I moved to Edmonton in 1981.

In Edmonton, I started getting into MDA, acid, mushrooms, mescaline, and other weird drugs. I started hanging out with a street hooker, and we dressed up in drag together. Guys would think I was a woman. I was young, I still didn't have to shave. It wasn't about sex. It was about trying to pass as a woman, and getting away with it.

I met many street people and learned some street lingo. I started doing ever more drag and ever more drugs. One day when I was nineteen or twenty, I couldn't remember what my boy name was. In response, I cut off the nails and hair and returned home to Calgary. I took six months or so to dry out in the basement. I decided that this is not where I'm heading, not what I want to do. I don't need to con people.

Following my return to Calgary, I rebuilt my old friendships and gained a hundred more. Calgary has always been very stable for me. It's my ground and I'll probably live there forever. It's the "big onion"—a city so nice it makes you want to cry.

It took me about a year to decide I wanted to do drag in the bar. At a local gay bar, I learned blocking, lighting, and sound. I got a lot of stage experience, and I started backing up accomplished drag performers. I began getting my own shows in 1985. That was really fun and I realized I was headed for a career in drag. I wanted to be on stage. I was painfully shy until I starting doing drag in Calgary, and it really turned me around. We started doing productions like *Grease*, *Chorus Line*, and *Cabaret*. After 1987, it became my responsibility to put things together and choreograph shows. I was really happy because that was what I wanted to do.

Still, it's amazing how many people hit on you when you're in drag. They don't want the person that is behind the drag, they want the person in drag. I don't take anybody home and leave my wig on. I've never actually gone home with anyone while I was in drag unless I knew them and I had already slept with them. There is no interest on my part if they want a transvestite or a transsexual.

In my career to date, I have performed hundreds of different characters while in drag. They're not all celebrities, but they're my impersonation or my interpretation of them. For example, my stage name has its own character. Marissa is a lounge-singer bubble head, and she's a comedian. So I might do Marissa as Norma Desmond, or I might do Carol Burnett's Gloria Swanson. I haven't done Lang lately. That's another one. A man impersonating a lesbian who dresses like a man. So it's a parody on a parody.

The drag queen organization includes many lesbigays[44] and straights who are not drag queens. I'm still part of the organization, although I've petered out in the last five years, and lost interest.

If you were wondering, let me be clear: I don't want to be a woman. I am happy being a gay man. "I'm a man in a dress with a dink" is my philosophy when I'm out. A drag queen is simply a man who dresses up. If somebody says, "You're such a great woman," I've done it right. After fifteen years, I should be doing it right.

The difference between a drag queen and a female impersonator is money. Female impersonators get paid for a gig, and in general, drag queens provide free volunteer shows or perform in fundraisers. Drag queens often call me a female impersonator. I have been a professional female illusionist in events like the Fringe Festival, for example.

There is a wide scope to drag, and everyone does it for different reasons. There are drag queens that do it for attention. There are some that will do it and take their teeth out, and some older guys who don't really strive to look like a woman. They just want to be silly, have fun, and entertain. I think a lot of guys do drag to hide their ugly male self. If they don't like themselves, they use drag to make themselves look prettier. That is not a healthy phenomenon. Some drag queens get off on the underwear. They're more like transvestites. There are others who grow boobs and have a dink, and they want to be half-and-half. Most guys who get the breast implants or the hormones and stuff don't actually pursue surgery.

The way I see it, the difference between drag and leather is that leather is more sexual for leathermen than drag is for drag queens. In another sense, they are both forms of drag in that they are both costumes, although uniform may be a better word to describe a leatherman's outfit. I think it has something to do with wanting to feel or look butch and masculine—then you do leather. If you want to experience your girl side, then you do drag. So they're part and parcel of the same thing, but they're different. I would say these forms of costume are part of gay identity.

For me, drag is about entertainment. It's fun to dress up. When I'm Marissa, I'm still me, and I still act like me. I don't throw attitude, and I'm not bitter, unless that is part of the character I'm impersonating. Even if I'm dressed as that character, when my performance is done, I go back to acting like myself. That's where I'm at with it. I like being gay and male. I like having a wiener. I like gay men, and I'm not attracted to women. It's fun to dress up, but that's about it.

I wouldn't wish drag on my best friend or my worst enemy because it's really hard. It's very competitive. Not so much here but it is competitive if you're going to be on a circuit and entertain and perform.

Do drag queens get stigmatized within the gay community? Definitely. It doesn't matter how hard you try, because you're still going to get criticized. Gay people tend not to hit: instead they talk and talk. They can stab you in the back with their words, rather than with an actual knife. There is always chatter and gossip and misconstrued stories and traumas. I find fags like to be catty and they like to be tacky, but there's a limit. It's not about hurting people's feelings.

The only harassment I've experienced is from rude taxi drivers. Once, when a driver realized my friend and I were guys, he sped up and drove dangerously fast and we said, "You know, we don't have to be here *yesterday*!" We got out of his car feeling shaken, but we were okay. He wasn't shouting anything at us, but he was glaring at us in his rearview mirror. I find that a lot of cab drivers are like that once you tell them you're going to a gay bar. Then it's like, "I got fags in the car!"

I don't need to show most people that I am gay. When I meet new people and they ask me, I tell them truthfully. If they don't ask, then I don't bring it up. I don't think it's important. I'm an "in-and-out" fag. I'm not into participating in pride marches and stuff either. It's just not me. I agree that we need to be heard and such, but I don't push it. I don't ram it down people's throats, because I see no need for that. I don't disagree with the ones that are loud, but I'm not a loud person as far as being gay. It's not how I operate or how I work.

I also need to learn how to be in a relationship. I know how to get along with people, but I have to learn how to be more open with my feelings toward a loved one.

I've never had a lover. I've had many boyfriends, but I've never actually had a lover. I've never gone with anyone for more then a month. I would define a lover as someone I would live with and be with for at least a year.

I think the problem is that no guy wants to be called "Mr. Marissa." Marissa is my stage name when I am in drag, and my friends will say something like, "Here comes Marissa and Marissa's boyfriend." They don't have their own name, they have my name. It's like Elizabeth Taylor's husband is Elizabeth Taylor's husband. Many guys don't want to deal with that and nor do I expect it of them. They want to be who they are.

I'm very independent, and a lot of people can't keep up to me. I have numerous projects: I'm doing a calendar, I'm planning a show, I'm doing choreography, I'm making a tape. I always have these things, plus drawing and painting. Consequently, I'm not ready for a lover. I'm not ready to settle down and get married. Maybe when I'm sixty-five I'll get together with someone.

I have been in love once. He was only interested in being my friend, however. We never got together sexually. We had coffee, we painted, we chatted, we had fun. He was my dream guy. It really hurt when he passed away.

I think everybody is going to answer your question differently about what is a gay positive identity. I just am a positive identity. I don't think of it as gay or straight. Gay doesn't rule my life. I am, so I'm fine with that. When I meet you, I won't go, "Hi, I'm gay." I'll go, "Hi, I'm Cliff. And you might as well know my other name is Marissa, because you are going to hear someone call me that."

I think just being happy and being friendly and nice to people is positive for a gay situation of any kind. If you are generally easygoing, happy, and content with what you're doing, and you're who you are, then no one can shoot you down. No one can say that you're doing the wrong thing because you're the one who has to look in the mirror in the morning. It's you who you have to face.

Paul, 50

It was difficult being gay at first, but I finally realized who I really was and that I loved myself enough to accept myself. That's when I knew everything would become easier. When I made the break, I made the break. In August 1986, I got all three of my kids together and told them all at once.

They looked at me and said, "Well, is that all you had to tell us, Dad?" I said, "Well, yeah," and they looked at me and said, "Well, then, can we go out and spend the day together?" I'm thinking to myself, "What's wrong with this picture?" They were a lot more accepting than I expected. That had been my one concern because they meant a lot to me. I moved on to telling the rest of the family and got what I figured I would get from them.

My one brother, a Jehovah Witness, said, "That's not the way God wants things. You're nothing but this, that, and everything else." I said, "Well, there's only one problem, John. That's what you are, too, and you're only hiding behind your religion with it." He replied that he is cured, and I told him there's no cure for this. We haven't talked in over twelve years now.

Fred, my other brother, and I have had our differences because he's a real redneck. At one point most of my family started believing various lies promulgated by my ex-wife. When my eldest son married, for example, Fred said, "You know, Paul, the only thing that I can't understand is why you didn't want your children." I said, "Hold it here a minute, I never said I did not want my children. If I don't want my children, why am I putting on a wedding, why do I have my daughter living with me, and why is my other son moving in with me? Does that sound like somebody who doesn't want their children?"

We had a talk there and that was that. I never heard from him again until fall 1996, when my daughter got married. Fred called me and told me that he decided I am still his brother, and although he may not agree with my lifestyle, he shouldn't judge it. He and I are still talking, but it's never going to be that true brotherly relationship that we once had.

I think my sister Charlene wants to accept me, but I think she is being pressured by my mother not to. Whatever she decides is fine with me.

My youngest son is also gay. When my daughter got married, my son and I went to see my mom because she was unable to attend the wedding. We fought because she felt she had a son, not a "daughter," and a grandson, not a "granddaughter." That was her mentality. I felt disappointed in her at that moment.

Later that day I met with Charlene and told her, "I love myself enough to walk away from it all today and not let it bother me. I have my partner and I have my children. If the rest of you don't want to be in my life, that's your decision. I am not giving up my life for you. I love myself enough to be who I really am. I thought that is what everybody wants out of life: for their family and loved ones to be honest with each other."

The only discrimination that I recall experiencing is having lost a job because they found out I was gay. It was done in a subtle and quiet way. I just chalked that up to small minds. I don't have time for that in my life.

Today I know my feelings are normal because they are my feelings; they are nobody else's. Becoming able to accept my feelings helped me become much more positive toward my sexuality. Now I don't have a problem with who knows that I'm gay. If I tell somebody and they don't happen to like it, I say goodbye.

Over the past eleven years, my life has been wonderful, other than some family bullshit. From the time I met Roger, I couldn't have asked for a better life. When I met him, I had no intentions of ever having another relationship, none whatsoever. I did not want one. I met him on May 12, 1986, and on June 1, we started living together. That's the way it happened. We had talked about it before that, but I kept saying, "No, I'm not doing it." Our feelings were just too strong, however, so we decided to take a chance with each other.

Meeting Roger was like meeting someone I had known all my life. There were fireworks. The connection between us was incredible. I didn't know I had the feelings within me that I felt for him. I was in shock the first night I went to his place because he had some of the same furniture in his bedroom that I had in mine. I wondered, what the hell is going on here? When I left that night, I cried all the way home. I knew that night that I was falling in love with him.

I wouldn't trade him for all the tea in China. There is no way. Our relationship is the best thing that ever happened to me. I've talked to my kids about it and I asked them, "Would you have rather seen Mom and I stay together?" Both said no. Then I asked, "Would you rather see me with a woman?," and they said, "No, Dad. We have never seen you so happy." My kids have all accepted Roger. As far as they're concerned, he is their stepfather. What more would I want out of life? I already have everything I value.

Roger never married. He has been openly gay all his adult life. Roger assumed that in a gay relationship, you need to put up with a lot of crap. We have had our differences, like in any relationship, gay or straight, but I told him that there is no difference between a gay relationship and a straight relationship. We all face the same problems. You have to work at it if you want it to work. You have to be able to communicate with one another, talk things out, and go forward from there. The only difference is that gay people have to worry about society and what they think about us. I told him that I couldn't care less what they think about me.

I am in a relationship, and I'm happy where I'm at. If you can't accept that, that's not my problem anymore. There are no games with me. The biggest thing to me about positive gay identity is accepting yourself and loving yourself. You're never going to find happiness in a relationship unless you do love yourself, because you have to know what love is before you can give it.

On July 4, 1987, Roger and I experienced a holy union ceremony together at the chapel on the university campus. Basically we got married. We had a professional photographer, and the reception was back at our place. We had a three-tiered wedding cake and everything. I had asked Roger if he would marry me, and he said yes. I felt that I really wanted to make a total commitment to him, and he wanted to as well. It was an absolutely wonderful day, with over fifty people present, half gay and half straight.

Roger was tested for the HIV virus in August 1987. He pre-warned me that if the results came back positive, I would have to leave. I just looked at him and said, "Pardon me. I'm going to tell you this right now: there is no way in this world that I would ever leave you over this. If you decided to run, I would take every penny I ever made to find you."

Unfortunately, the results came back positive. I was myself diagnosed as HIV positive in November 1988. He blamed himself for giving me the virus. I said, "Nobody knows where we got it from. I don't know it and you don't know it." We had not practiced safer sex because, back in 1986, safer sex was not yet a big issue. It was still the beginning of HIV awareness. I decided that there was no possible way that I would be negative about Roger's HIV status. At first Roger thought he would be dead in six months. On our tenth anniversary, I said, "Well Roger, it's been a long six months, hasn't it?"

What matters to me is dealing with this and making the best of my life. There is no point in dwelling on the fact that I am HIV positive and that I'm going to die. My theory is that you are born to die, and each day you have is one day less. Nonetheless, my HIV status does not mean I'm dying.

I've been more conscious of living since 1972, when I almost did die. I think there is too much emphasis put on where I got the virus. I don't really give a shit because I think whatever the good Lord wants me to die from is what I'm going to die from. There is a reason for it.

My physician at times had a hard time dealing with me because I was so nonchalant. She said, "Paul, you don't seem to be upset." I replied, "What is there to be upset about? I was dying yesterday. Just because I'm HIV positive doesn't mean I'm going to die from AIDS. I could walk out of here today, get hit by a bus, or fall down the stairs and break my neck and die! Does that mean I died from AIDS?"

I doubt that HIV is something that just sprung up in 1984. What is AIDS? It's pneumonia and quick cancer for most people. Well, pneumonia and cancer have been around for how many years?

To date I have not had any symptoms, other than that my T4 count[45] has gone down. But you know what? It's only a number, that's all it is. I'm a positive type of person. I do not believe in sitting around and dwelling on the challenges I face. It doesn't make matters better for you. It only makes things worse for you because you pull yourself down emotionally.

Regarding my own growth as a gay person, I've fully arrived at where I'm at with who I am. I would like the uneducated to realize that we are not child molesters or perverts. Some are, but they exist in every walk of life. We're no different from anyone else. I have found happiness, but it's all because I found happiness within myself and learned to love myself.

John, 61

I was not able to come out to my father before he passed away, but I did come out to my mother before her death. She was wonderful. Although she could be snobbish, she really was an elegant lady. When I told her, she was amazingly accepting, I think partly because she always loved me, and partly because she was proud of me. I also think my father would have been accepting, although disappointed. Unlike my mother, my father was not snobbish at all. He felt that we can all learn from everybody and some people are more privileged in life than others. He never looked down on people who were less privileged.

In any event, I guess I've answered the question initially about how I embarked on this journey toward being a positive gay person and feeling positive about myself. First, I established a good relationship with my children and second, I was able to carry on within my profession in a very positive way. My profession led me into some very positive appointments to various committees and boards and so forth, where it was known that I was a gay person.

I have been involved with a federal political party over the last twenty-eight years. A former prime minister knew that I was gay, and he was well aware of my accomplishments. At the time, I had undertaken some major responsibilities for this party, and the prime minister let me know that I had a place in the party. He had a positive attitude toward gay people.

At a small dinner party for several high-ranking-party members, I took the opportunity to say that I was proud to be a member of this political party, since I felt it is an inclusive party, rather than an exclusive party. I went on to say that I was one of those people in the invisible minority who felt comfortable within the party. I received a standing ovation for my comments and the leader of the party came over and shook my hand.

I don't want to give you the impression that being gay has been easy, however. I was physically attacked about fifteen years ago, walking on a beautiful summer evening with a friend. We were wearing white pants and colorful shirts. I think my friend had his hand over my shoulder or something, and we decided to walk to the gay bar. Three drunken bums attacked us and beat us up severely.

I was on the ground and bleeding when some people came along and ended the attack. I went directly down to the police station and the police were very sympathetic. Several days later the police contacted me and said, "We have found the people who attacked you, but why didn't you tell us you were gay?"

Apparently these assailants claimed that we had attacked them, and they were going to lay charges against us if we pursued this. In court, it would be a question of whom the judge would believe. Keep in mind that these guys were absolute bums. Nevertheless, because we were gay, we were second-class citizens in the eyes of the police. Consequently, they were not interested in prosecuting the thing at all.

I do not regret the fact that I was once married and had children. One reason for my positive feelings about being gay is my increasingly close relationship with my children. The older they have grown, the closer we have become. The incredible endorsement by my children has been a major factor for me.

Another reason I do not regret my marriage is that I met some nice people through my wife, including her own family. Her sister has been incredibly nice to me since the marriage break-up. I could always talk to her when I couldn't talk to my wife. She has been absolutely fabulous.

The only continuing unhappiness for me in my firm has been with one man, who became the managing partner. I felt he was totally homophobic and once he took over, I noticed that I was getting no new work from him. Any major new work that came into the firm went to a partner who was junior to me by fifteen years. On a comparative performance basis, eventually you don't look as good as those who are getting important assignments. That's really the only negative thing that has happened at my firm. I intend to retire in three years, and I will soon be discussing my retirement plan with some of my partners.

I have been in a relationship with Aziz for eleven years in Canada, after initially meeting him in Africa fourteen years ago. We have developed a positive gay relationship. If I could take a needle today that would make me straight tomorrow, I don't think I would. If I were twenty and starting to article again at my law firm, though, I might.

The one thing I still need to do to continue my development as a gay man is to get involved in educating straight people. I have seriously thought about writing an autobiography. My children have encouraged me to do it. It would be either a short story or a book on what it's like to be gay in North America: what we've had to put up with, what we have achieved, what we have come through, and where we're at now. I want to educate straight people that we, as gay people, are very much like they are, have much the same set of values in many areas, and that we are part of the same world in which they grew up.

One topic we have not discussed is the subject of sexual behavior. I went to a play recently in which certain scenes suggested that gay men were having sex in a park. It's not that I'm in anyway judgmental, but having this seedy scene in the play was embarrassing to me. Some of my straight friends had accompanied me to the play and felt the same way.

One type of gay person that I do not like is the type that makes outrageous public statements and behaves in an attention-seeking manner. I would find it equally distasteful to see a heterosexual woman flaunting herself in an unbecoming manner. I do not respect people who are totally irresponsible.

I believe that I am a good example of a gay individual who has succeeded, despite the odds. I have come a long way from when I married and rejected one side of myself to where I am today. I see myself as a positive example to younger gay people that they can get on with their lives and make all kinds of contributions in many areas and spheres of life, whether it's becoming chair of the United Way or a local AIDS organization, or whether it's becoming a priest in a church. I think those kinds of gay people are to be respected.

David, 16

Although I am still a virgin, I think often about sex. I eventually want to have sex with the right person. I am a person who likes to be committed to somebody and deeply involved, whether it's a friendship or a relationship. I like friends who know me deeply. I think I will eventually fall in love with a man who is as sensitive as I am and someone who really cares about who they are.

I think that having casual sex with different people might be interesting, but you need to think about your life. With HIV and AIDS out there, it might be dangerous. Besides the danger, I've also wondered if perhaps the emotional attachment isn't there if you have casual sex. It can cause big problems, too, if you really like that person but they don't like you that much. Then you go your separate ways and you're still wanting this person. That's what I don't think I would like about casual sex. I think you should be more involved and more committed to each other before you start having intimate sexual relations.

I've often felt that marriages for gay couples should be permitted. I believe that this would provide a sense of having greater equality with the straight community, but it would also provide a sense of closure within a relationship. You wouldn't always have to consider your partner to be merely your boyfriend.

To continue my development as a gay male, I need to make more gay friends and acquaintances, and get involved in more community activities...those that I can join at my age. It's difficult because most of them are for older individuals, and they either don't allow younger people to get involved or they just aren't something that would interest me. I will get involved in whatever I can in the community that is applicable to me. It would also be nice if I wasn't as sensitive to criticism. It bothers me when other people make cruel jokes, for example, about gay people. I want to believe that that's okay, this is who I am, so that's their problem.

I still feel strange with the behavior of some gay people. Sometimes they are too crass. That really shocks me. I'll be standing there thinking, "How could you say that?" I'm still uncomfortable with some activities in the gay community as well, but I'm really getting to see the positive side of who we are.

My hope is that society will become more accepting of gay people in general, and that they'll be taught that we aren't monsters or aliens. I also hope that young people will become educated about gays while they're still most impressionable about those types of things. I believe it should begin in grade five as part of sex education.

I think my acceptance will grow as I continue to become more comfortable with myself. I'm sure I have a lot of growing to do yet. I used to think, "Oh my God, I'm gay, I don't want to be gay." Now the thought of being straight seems so boring to me.

Glenn, 46

I came out to my friends before telling my family, and that was a positive experience. It really scared me to come out to my London friend, Brian, and his wife June. June's response was that it's not who you love that is important, but rather who you are as a person. Brian was totally accepting. I am now very open with him about leather, too.

I came out to my family in 1990. The build-up to it was frightening. I was in a relationship, and I couldn't make it to family functions when I was invited, or I couldn't do this or that because of commitments within the relationship. I was becoming a nervous wreck. I took an afternoon off work and went to tell my parents. Their reaction was not what I expected. My parents were supportive, positive, and accepting. I think my father accepted it quicker than my mother. Even today, I think my mother is concerned about the possibility of my contracting AIDS.

Let me tell you more about the leather scene. Walking into a leather bar can be scary. There is a strong feeling of anxiety mixed with anticipation. Initially, there can be a great deal of distance maintained between patrons; everybody's guard seems to be up. As the evening progresses, the guys become more relaxed with each other. Leather bars are usually fairly dark. Their atmosphere creates an aura of mystery, frequently with a dungeon theme. There's a lot of posing and a lot of cruising.

There is a close bond among men who are into the leather scene. Love and trust are a big part of it. Most of the people I have met are stable, intelligent, trustworthy people. Some have been very lonely as well, though. It's not all that it's cracked up to be.

The leather community is part of the greater gay community at large, but we're still seen as something different. I enjoy the uniqueness that comes from belonging to one of the community's subgroups.

One author has called the leather scene a celebration of death. I don't agree. I think it's a celebration of life. Yes, there are aspects of power and masculinity in it, but I look at it more from the aspect of eroticism. I have probably been attracted to leather since I can remember. The color, the shine, the smell and the allure are a turn-on for me. Men are extremely visual, and there is a heavy visual impact in wearing leather garments. Clothes of any kind can be very erotic, especially during initial physical contact, like necking and groping scenes. I prefer to "play" fully or partially clothed in leather because I like the tactile aspect of it and the look of it. If you've ever listened to the sound of another man remove his leather clothing in the dark, it can be arousing. From the research I've done, one man in every twenty has a fetish for something.

Valerie Steele, in her book *Fetish*, describes five levels of fetishism. Five is where you can't achieve orgasm without your fetish. I'm probably at a two. I don't have to wear leather to have an orgasm or sexual satisfaction, but it is nice.

Men who are into leather are very much into masculinity. Any garment that conveys masculinity may become an interest or a fetish, like jockstraps, for example. Many guys are into that. In the age of AIDS, one should be careful about criticizing leather, because the aim is to heighten the erotic experience of sex; when you're into leather, there's so much more you can do besides fucking. Fantasies can become realities. I have been in leather scenes where neither of us had an orgasm, became naked, nor exposed ourselves. My biggest sex organ is between my ears. I believe it is a special love to be with somebody and offer them the gift of freedom to explore aspects of their sexuality that they probably have a yearning to explore but haven't yet found the right outlet for.

When you get into things like leather play, power dynamics are enacted. That is what many people call "S&M."[46] These labels don't apply, however. Leather sex is consensual—it is not about inflicting pain. Leather sex is intended to be pleasurable and mutually fulfilling for both parties.

Generally, there are defined roles. One partner is the top (i.e., dominant) and one is the bottom (i.e., passive). Those roles are assigned through trust. My role is generally that of the top, but I cannot be that without the consent of the bottom, and the bottom cannot be the bottom without my consent. The leather community lives by the motto "Safe, sane, and consensual."

Leather sex is done within an etiquette, within rules and guidelines. The rules are set up so that nobody gets hurt. Often, the bottom is given a code word or a gesture that he can use whenever things get out of hand or when he reaches a limit that it is no longer pleasurable for him. If someone is in a scene where he is being hurt physically or mentally, it's time to blow the whistle and stop. Continuing is not healthy for anybody.

A typical scene for me is about control and domination. It's fantasy and it's role-playing. The role-playing is probably very healthy, in that I do not feel that I have much control or power in my daily life. I've had partners who do have power and control in their daily lives, and when we get together, we can switch roles, do some playacting, and get it out of our system. It is a release. I don't want to hurt anybody. I inflict pleasure, not pain. What good is a sexual partner who's hurting?

When we get talking about which things are feminine and which are masculine, I get lost in that debate. Both are human. I can't say that being into leather is a total rejection of femininity, and I can't say that being into drag is a complete rejection of masculinity either. I know people who are into both and those who are in between. Leathermen can swish as much as drag queens.

When leathermen develop relationships, the power dynamics

enjoyed sexually do not usually permeate the relationship itself, unless the partners involved design their relationship with that in mind. Differences exist in all relationships. For example, I know of relationships where there is a disparity between income and levels of education. It's up to the couple involved to deal with their unique set of power differences and find their own solutions.

Leather relationships are like any relationship: there are many things that need to be negotiated and agreed upon. We still have to go through the relationship dynamics of being in love and settling in and making the adjustment to live together. My friends in the leather community live normal lives like everybody else.

If anybody wants to sit and talk to me about the leather community, my time is always available. As a responsible leatherman, it is my obligation to educate. I feel that I am open enough that I see the gay community as a whole, rather than as fragmented parts. Don't forget that underneath, the leatherman is a human being.

I have never really felt that I have suffered any discrimination. I've never been bashed either. I used to experience a lot of comments like, "Hey, fag!" from passing cars, but I don't now that I'm older.

As for my continuing development as a gay man, I've had two relationships, one good and one bad, and I think that this aspect of my life is now integrated. There really isn't a lot more work that I need to do, except the normal things in life that are going to start happening because I'm getting older. I've had to deal with a difficult midlife crisis, for example, which had nothing to do with being gay.

As an aside, I really dislike the emphasis that North American gay male culture places on youth and beauty. In places like Holland, for example, the older gay man is sought after as much as the young pretty boy.

Another issue that is coming to fore is that I am of the generation devastated by AIDS. I have fewer and fewer friends my own age. When I go to the bar, I notice that there are many people younger than I am and many who are older. I continue to face the prospect of seeing close friends wither away and die. That is a serious concern.

When I first came out, I went through a phase of feeling that being gay was almost everything. I wore all the buttons and the badges. I was into volunteer work here, there, and everywhere. I went to bars and did the whole scene. Recently at a cross-cultural workshop, a model called the identity flower was presented. Each petal on the flower represents something about you: where you were born, where you grew up, the language you speak, your gender, and so on. All these things together form a flower. That's where I'm at now in terms of positive gay identity; being gay is merely one petal on the flower, and that is a part of the whole. It's no more or no less important than any other aspect of who I am. I think this is a healthy view of identity.

We can become dreadfully lost in the gay issue. I can become an extremely radical gay person when I want to be, and that particular petal on the flower then becomes prominent. By and large, however, it's just a part of me right now. I can be as open about it as I want to be, as I can with any aspect of myself. Being gay is really no big deal. Being so heavily into leather is no big deal. There's a hell of a lot more to me than what you see. I try to look at the whole person when I meet people. You can't make surface judgments on one thing.

One needs to build a positive gay identity because the coming-out process never ends. You're always going places and meeting new people. The important issue for me is self-acceptance. Essentially I strive to be a good person. I am an intelligent, educated, aware, productive, taxpaying member of society. I am an integral part of the culture and the political process of the society in which I live. I feel that I deserve all the rights and privileges in society accorded to everybody else. Fighting for that right will cause the gay petal on my flower to become larger and more important if the situation allows. Above all, I am a human being with human issues. I also happen to be gay.

Troy, 24

I thought a lot about your question of how I came to adopt a positive gay identity. I came out when I was going on twenty-three, at which point I felt that I had matured sufficiently. I've noticed that gay teenagers who are out are confused. Combined with the ordinary challenges of adolescence, their struggle seems overwhelming. I've observed a number of them flunk out of school. I always thought if I had come out five years earlier, I would have been in so much trouble. I think I would have become totally promiscuous.

At age twenty-three, in fact, I felt ready for a relationship, and it didn't take me long to feel comfortable with Warren. I was infatuated initially, but now I am in love with him. I want to be with him for a long time. Compared to how I felt toward Jodine earlier, this seemed like miles apart. I felt an overwhelming certainty. There was no doubt, everything felt right.

I only came out to my dad in August. I really didn't know how it was going to go, and I was pretty scared. He said, "Well, this isn't what I wanted, this isn't what I dreamed of, but I still love you." I gave him a book to read because he's not easy to talk to. Even after I told him, a week later I had dinner with him, and it didn't come up in conversation. I felt like saying, "What are you thinking? What's going on in your head?" There still isn't any talk about it. Although I knew he wouldn't receive it well, I was tired of lying and pretending. I was tired of answering the "Any new girlfriend?" question. I think it's going to take him awhile.

I had a decent upbringing so I turned out okay because of that. I'm really lucky that I had great parents. I also feel that I had my head on my shoulders by the time I came out. A good upbringing and positive parenting are the two factors I think had the most to do with my development of a positive gay identity. That has affected the people I hung out with, the things I did, and my outlook on life. For example, my mom is my biggest supporter, and she has been since the day I told her. I have not had a bad experience with anyone that I have come out to. It has all been very positive. I think my positive gay identity just grew out of me being a positive person and a decent person.

One thing I still struggle with is the influence of my dad and my dad's family. They're image conscious and conservative, which has had an affect on what I'm like as well. To an extent this is a positive thing, but to another extent it is not. My mother is carefree and unconcerned about image. I can see the advantage of both approaches.

I would like to learn more about gay history, literature, and the arts. I would also like to become more politically active. Something I am dealing with now in my development as a gay man is the whole dynamic of a gay relationship, and the trust factor. I think we're bombarded by the stereotype that gay men are pigs and sluts. Consequently, I find it difficult to trust. Warren is living in Ontario, and I am here in Edmonton attending university. We don't express it as such to each other, but because it is a long-distance relationship, the issue of fidelity is there. I think about my relationship a lot and where it will be in the future. I hope it will survive the temporary distance.

Andrew, 29

Within six months of living in Edmonton, I had started living an openly gay life. I felt like I had arrived and was totally ready. I began disclosing to several people at law school. Within a couple of months, the Alberta Human Rights Commission held a panel discussion at the law faculty. I felt totally comfortable standing up and talking about my experience as a gay man living in Alberta in front of all my peers. I couldn't have done that two months earlier.

Nothing was ever said to my face, but I think some of my peers became more distant from me after that. The people that I was close to became closer, however. Some of my relationships with faculty changed, too, but that may have had more to do with the fact that my focus on studying was somewhat diverted because of my night job in a gay bar. I think I became more honest with myself and if I didn't like something, I spoke up. I suspect that changed my relationship with some faculty as well.

When I first moved to Edmonton, I still wasn't comfortable going into a gay bar, so I decided that a perfect job would be to work in one, to confront that fear. I thought of the bar as a safe gay environment where I would meet gay people. I landed a job in a gay bar and spent the first two months with my jaw hanging to the ground, absolutely shocked. My learning curve was incredible, and I was soon ready to explore.

My experience there helped me to better understand gay stereotypes. I decided that the totally over-the-top hairdressers and out gay men were incredibly honest, exciting, interesting, fun, and full of original thought. I think what made those people fun and interesting was their comfort level with themselves and their acceptance of gay culture and the world in which they live. Alternatively, the straight-looking, straight-acting gays seemed uncomfortable with their bodies, their selves, and their environment. I didn't find them genuine.

I wondered if straight-acting gays are simply playing a role, but I don't think it's so cut and dry. Some straight-acting gays seem deathly afraid that their families and work will find out they're gay. The only place that they're really gay is at the bar. Perhaps after several drinks, they find a man, and that's it. The next day, they're back in their other life. That's at one extreme. Then there are gays who seem to accept their gayness and don't hide it, but they still live straight lives outside of their gay lives. At the other extreme are people who live, eat, breathe, and sleep their gayness. They are immersed in being gay, like as a culture. I don't think that either extreme is healthy.

The immersion thing happened for me while I worked in the gay bar. While I was there, I think I lost a really important chunk of the rest of my community—like straight friends and school friends. There was a period of about a year-and-a-half where I don't think I did much socially with people who weren't gay. It was an important time for me, though, as I learned a lot about myself and a lot about gay culture.

Readiness is an important point here. My disclosure to others and my immersion did not occur until I was in a place of power, where the cost wouldn't outweigh the benefit. When I started learning about my history as a gay man, it had a lot to do with my development and my identification with gay politics. When I began to question gay political issues and think of them for myself, I started thinking about the way we're portrayed in media and the limited access that gay youth have to positive images and role models.

At the end of that process, I felt ready to come out to my mom and dad. I was twenty-six. They no longer had power over me by blaming it on Karen. I talked to Karen about it beforehand, and then I realized that they'd done so much growing as parents of gay children that it wouldn't be an issue anymore.

My mom came out to visit, followed by my dad. I disclosed to Mom, and it filled the gap in our relationship. It felt really good to bring her up to speed on the experiences in my life. It was almost cathartic.

When Dad arrived, I told him. His reaction was couched in terms of real concern for me, for my future, and my ability to practice law and have a meaningful existence in a discriminatory world. He's very cerebral and articulate, and less in touch with feeling. He accepted my disclosure in an almost resigned way. I thought that was the end of it until last Christmas.

John and I had been together for about a year already. I was finally with a partner I envisioned being with for the rest of my life. That was the first time that had happened. I wanted my parents to meet him, and we planned on going to my parents' home for Christmas. Mom and Karen were happy about the prospect, but when Dad found out, he hit the roof. He basically said that it wasn't going to happen.

I was very angry, hurt, and offended by this. With Karen he's arrived, but he still hangs onto a perception that sex between men is dirty. My father continues to have really negative stereotypes and visions of gay male sexuality. I was disappointed in this reaction, but I've gotten over my anger. Until he meets a partner of mine and realizes that gay men are not all flaming queens, I don't think he will break his negative stereotypes. I don't think he can get there on his own. Nonetheless, telling Dad was like the closing of a chapter. I would now be better able to integrate being gay into the rest of my life.

John and I broke up this past spring after being together for fifteen months. Mom was incredibly supportive in all the ways that a mother can be. I think she now sees my partner as a person I've chosen to spend my life with as opposed to viewing him as a gender or an orientation. My dad is not there yet.

When I entered law school, I knew that I wanted to study law and that it wasn't necessarily about *practicing* law. However, the fact that the law profession is incredibly homophobic has something to do with the fact that I'm not there and I'm not practicing it. My work environment now is incredibly supportive, and the work is very meaningful to me. The fact that I did not want to article, and have not articled, has something to do with my decision to be an out gay man. I won't let go of the power that gives me personally. I would need to practice law and exist in that profession on my own terms. Finding a comfortable place for me and my sexuality in the larger world is an ongoing challenge, but less so every day.

I've certainly been a victim of emotional violence and verbal harassment, but I have never been assaulted or discriminated against in a really obvious way. I also am aware that any number of jobs or opportunities may not have been offered to me because there was either the perception or the knowledge that I was gay. I have no idea if I didn't get a summer job at a law firm because I have an air or appearance of being gay, or if it was because my résumé reflects my gay journey. My attributions for why things have happened may be completely different from why they actually happened. I do have a fear of violence, and some of my friends have been severely assaulted. That has a direct effect on my personal relationships and on my social and political identity.

In this short interview, I can't do justice to some of the incredible loneliness and feelings of despair that I've gotten over. Because I've left those behind, I think I've really built a wall around them. They were most prevalent during my teenage years. It was more than being denied romantic interests or pursuing contact with men. It was more about being isolated from a community and an identity. These feelings had a social context. The loneliness was about having no culture around me that reflects the sexual part of my identity. There was then no way to be validated as a gay person. Although I had access to some validation from a gay sibling who developed personal power, it wasn't mine, and I didn't feel like I could grab hold of it and own it. It wasn't there for me.

This undercurrent of isolation continued until I had control and power in my life in other ways—like financial independence, career direction, and the identity and ownership that comes in your life with being away from home. Once I had that power over my life, the despair around sexuality for me almost disappeared. I knew there would be a time and place where I would arrive.

In my continuing development as a gay man, I think I need to accept the fact that I'm still somewhat homophobic. I need to find a balanced place for my sexuality and how it affects who I am in the rest of my life.

When I look at my current challenges as a gay man, I think one of my biggest is looking at how to integrate my gay identity into my overall sense of being. I did the immersion experience where everything I did was gay or gay related. It's been part of my journey. What's left for me is to integrate who I am into the rest of my life, so that my sexuality is a part of me that doesn't define me. Somewhere in the middle of that continuum is complete acceptance of who I am, but where being gay is not more important in defining me than the sports I enjoy, or my profession, for example.

Alex, 23

I really enjoyed being with Franklin, and I ended up moving in with him more permanently after the confrontation with my parents.

By this point, I was a flamer. I was hanging out with incredibly queer people, and I was beginning to get a sense of queer identity. I was also doing a lot of modeling for Franklin's fashion shows.

Every spring Franklin hosted a benefit, a fashion show, to help an AIDS organization. We wore black ties and arrived in a rented Rolls Royce. This begins the story of how I came out at school. As I got out of the car, a guy named Troy was waiting to greet us. He knew me from rugby and he was also in my English class. As the fashion show began and I appeared on the runway, the entire crowd cheered because they all knew me. I removed my robe, leaving my body clad in only a pair of boxer shorts. At sixteen, I had a six-pack stomach, and I was in great shape and tanned. The crowd cheered and yelled loudly. Troy sat there stunned.

I returned to school that Monday. As I walked into English class, there was complete silence. Everybody in the school already knew, but the only time I ever got any flack for being gay was from a grade-nine punk. He called me a faggot, so I lifted him up against the lockers and said, "Sorry, what did you say to me?"

"Nothing man, nothing."

"Just checking." That was the end of that.

I was on student council at the school and everybody knew me and liked me already, so being gay wasn't a big issue. I left that school shortly thereafter, however, because I wanted to go to a semestered school.

My friend Roger and I went to a school near our house and inquired into beginning there in the fall. The principal was completely atrocious. He called us faggots. Roger had a Caesar cut, and he wore makeup and a tight shirt with nipple rings showing through. We both wore earrings. The principal just didn't know how to handle us, and he said that it would be a cold day in hell before homosexuals started coming to his school. We went to the school board, and they forced him to let us in.

When Roger and I went to register, the principal warned us, "When the *real* students beat you up, don't come looking for pity here because you won't find any." He made us sign a contract saying that if we missed more than two classes, we would be expelled.

After I left that day, I decided I would not attend that school. That's when I started becoming more political. I called an adult supporter who had helped us get into the school and let her know what happened. We ended up holding a press conference. Roger and I spoke about how degrading and abusive this principal was. The school board responded by holding a forum on the topic of sexuality in schools, which later resulted in the principal's demotion. I was amazed at what we had accomplished.

Franklin wasn't all that amazed, however, because I wasn't in school and I wasn't working. Instead, I was going to the bar every night. He kicked me out. I couldn't go home, and I couldn't stay with friends.

I left for Ottawa and stayed in a shelter for kids because I didn't know where else to go. While I was there, I saw a poster for a protest on Parliament Hill about homelessness and homeless kids. By this point, I was pretty comfortable with being gay. I had been surrounded by gay people for just about a year. Everyone I knew was gay, everyone I talked to was gay, and everything I did was gay. I ate at gay restaurants, I went to gay bars, and I listened to gay music.

I went to the protest. Some neo-Nazis wanted to kill me because they knew I was a faggot. I challenged their leader, but Anne—the coordinator of the protest—came over and ended it. I decided to stay there all night with them because they were actually a pretty cool group. At about four in the morning, I asked Anne where these kids would end up tomorrow. She said she didn't know. Parliament Hill has a big lawn with stone gates right on the sidewalk. That night we slept on the sidewalk.

I returned the next night, and there were around seventy people who slept over. The next night there were about thirty-five kids there. A couple of days later, we decided we were going to stay and formed a collective. We bought a couple of blue tent tarps to put over us. This began in October, and by April, we had six tents and two extra tarps, with the entire compound surrounded in hay. One tarp was used to cover a kitchen, complete with a stove. We fed about a hundred and fifty people every day.

We stayed right through minus forty-degree weather. The bottom line is that we couldn't leave because there were so many kids counting on us to be there. About three hundred and fifty kids slept there throughout the winter. I slept indoors maybe ten nights out of the whole winter.

That was my first introduction to political involvement and speaking out. It was such an incredible experience. It introduced me to the whole theory of youth helping youth. No one was doing anything about street kids in Ottawa, so we did something for each other. We helped so many kids get off the street and into their own apartments.

I had become much more street-oriented than before. My jeans would get dirty and I wore the same socks for two or three days in a row. I wouldn't shower for a couple of days either. I wore my toque and my poncho, and I panhandled. A couple of times when our camp needed fuel for the heaters, I prostituted myself again. I was seventeen and still hustling.

Franklin and I had really become distant from each other. I was pretty gross at that point in my life. I wasn't taking care of myself, inside or outside. I was helping all these other people and not doing anything for myself. When the camp ended, I went to the hospital because I thought I was losing my mind.

Once I regained my health, I was hired by a group who traveled across Canada speaking out about violence and social justice issues. I started talking about my experiences being gay, homeless, and an addict to as many as fifteen hundred people at a time. I traveled across Eastern Canada doing that until the fall. I continued becoming more comfortable with being gay.

I was proud to be gay, and I was very happy. I believe the more comfortable I am with my sexuality, the more other people will be with theirs. We need to start talking about sexuality issues, including lesbigay teen issues. That's the only way our healing is going to start, both inside and outside ourselves.

At eighteen, I moved back to Vancouver and worked for an environmental organization. I began to totally identify with the gay area there. It was amazing to be in a place where I could be me and feel safe. I lived with Les, a guy who I had started seeing in Ottawa. He was totally cute and loveable. The relationship didn't work out very well, though, and he later moved to Nova Scotia. I was really hurt because this had been my first equitable gay relationship.

At that point in my life, I realized that I wasn't going to walk into a bar and have all the men love me. When I was fifteen or sixteen, I could walk into any bar and have any man I wanted. When I walked into a bar in Vancouver, no one noticed me. I had to wait in line and pay the cover charge like everyone else. I was not the prize anymore. Being in Vancouver was definitely not a confidence booster.

I moved to Edmonton in November 1994 and got a job working with street kids. This is when my healing really started. I stopped drinking and I stopped smoking drugs. I have now abstained for over a year-and-a-half.

Since I've lived in Edmonton, I've had a couple of longer relationships. Longer means several months—one was five months and the other was eight months. I'm twenty-three now, and although I'm attracted to people physically who are my age, that's where it stops. I'm not into the bar scene anymore and I'm not much into one-night stands either. I'm mentally attracted to people who are in their late twenties. I try to date people my age, but I'm just not into them. I get frustrated being gay in Edmonton because if you want to meet someone here, you've got to frequent the bar. I know there are numerous social and political groups you can join, but even they seem work oriented to me, and I don't have the time or energy to go to meetings at night.

I now work fifty to sixty-five hours a week. My job is my priority in life. Relationships I've had since this job haven't been overly successful because I'm not looking for anything intense. I want something very casual, like let's get together once or twice a week, have dinner or whatever, and if it goes farther, then I'll re-evaluate my life.

Currently I am the executive director of a nonprofit agency that works with young people involved with child welfare and the youth justice system. Its mandate is to help youth start their own healing because the department of social services would like to think that you can give a kid a social worker and a therapist and healing with automatic results. That's not how it works. They've got to be in a space where they want to start healing and where they want to start talking about what happened when they were young and how it makes them feel. We incorporate the theory of youth helping youth. Young people listen to me and take direction from me because I have been there, and I am young. They connect with who I am and what I represent. The most amazing thing is that because I'm comfortable being gay, several kids have come out to me soon after meeting me. The way I look at it, the more comfortable I am with myself, the more comfortable other people will be with me as well.

I'm very proud of being gay. I'm planning to get a rainbow band tattooed on my arm with the word pride underneath. If I use any label, it would be queer. I live a relatively gay lifestyle, I support gay organizations, I shop in gay businesses, I support my community, but it's not in the forefront anymore. No longer do I need to walk down the mall and have people know that I'm gay.

I grew up in this gay world where gay clothing was tight and came from Le Chateau or Club Monaco. Now I don't want to wear a skin tight shirt on a Sunday afternoon. I'm at that point where I don't need that. I don't need to shave every day. This is who I am. I'm also a youth worker and a vegetarian. These are all parts of who I am.

I would never not want to be gay. There are days when I'm desperately single, and I would love to have someone to spend the night with to cuddle and watch a movie. I also have to remember that I am only twenty-three and I don't need to be getting married right now. I have several people that I can date here and there. That's where I'm at now in my life. I'm gay and this is who I am. I hope to help young people shape their identity, or at least shape their appreciation for who they are.

With respect to gay young people, I want them to know that it's all right. When a kid tells me "I think I might be gay," or "Hey, you know I hustled when I was younger," I already know it before the kid tells me. I can tell. I can meet a kid and know that within months he'll come to me and say, "Alex, I think I might be gay."

In my continuing development as a gay man, I am reconsidering what I want out of a relationship. Do I want to commit to someone or continue having these cheesy relationships that aren't going anywhere? I think I need to get into a long-term healthy relationship: one that's based on trust, respect, and understanding. Someone to share and grow with. I think when that occurs, that will be the pinnacle of my gay development. I want to be with a partner. It's the next step.

Being gay is about intimacy and supporting. It's who I love, it's not who I choose to love. I don't know if I've had true love yet. I know I've been in lust, and I've thought I've been in love at times. In hindsight, I'm not sure. I know the time will come when I'll meet someone and it's going to click. I don't doubt that at all. I'm attracted to men, I enjoy having sex with them, and the intimate part is not there for me with women.

Let me now tell you about some positive and negative highlights I've experienced in my gay journey. The gay pride march in New York in 1994 was completely amazing, for example. There were over a million gay people present. Marching in the Toronto Gay Pride Parade has also been exhilarating. Last summer, that parade even had more than a million in attendance. I wasn't there, but I heard the streets were packed. It was the first year that I haven't been involved. I've taken part in pride marches in Vancouver, New York, Calgary, Edmonton, Toronto, Montreal, Ottawa, and Halifax. I like to travel, and my goal is now to do the United States. I'm going to migrate to San Francisco for their pride march next year.

On the more negative side, when I attend the pride march in Calgary and see four hundred people marching in the rain, I find it disheartening. My happiness is geographically based, to some extent. It has nothing to do with who I am really. I get frustrated with the Alberta gay community. Gay people should vote for politicians who are going to make changes for us. I have the impression that either we don't vote, or we just go with the flow. That disgusts me.

There have been times when I've been harassed in the parking lots of gay bars across the country. I've had rocks thrown at me and stuff like that. I have been gay-bashed a couple of times too. The first assault occurred while I was ending a relationship in Ottawa. I was feeling very emotional, and I thought eating pizza might make me feel better. The pizza joint was closed, so I asked this guy standing outside when they closed and he looked at me and said, "*I don't know.*" I was wearing a button that said, "Boycott homophobia," and he noticed it and said, "What are you, a homosexual, or just a plain faggot?" I replied, "Fuck you!" He stood up and hit me. This guy was big, but I beat him up right there. As I left, I said, "You've had your ass kicked by a faggot." I walked away feeling good. I saw him a week later with his friends, and I was worried that he would kill me. Instead, he just walked by me and looked away.

The second assault occurred five months ago. I was walking out of a straight pool hall on First Street in Calgary, accompanied by a straight male friend and his girlfriend. Three drunk young guys, probably eighteen to twenty, were in front of us. One of them turned around and said to my female friend, "Are you looking at my ass?" She replied, "No, to be honest I wasn't." He retorted, "Oh, you fucking dyke," and then the three of them started chiming in: "Dyke, dyke, dyke." We left and headed toward a nearby gay bar. By the time we arrived, these same three guys were hitting a guy who was just leaving the bar with pipes. I got out of our vehicle and said, "Hey guys, what's going on?" They all stood up, ready to fight. I convinced them to walk away, but one of them looked back at my male friend and asked, "What did you say?" He hadn't said a thing. This hoodlum was about to hit my friend in the head with the pipe when I moved in to help. I grabbed his wrist and removed the pipe. Before leaving with his friends, he sucker punched the side of my face.

One of my saddest memories is thinking about the many people who have failed me in my life. When I called out for help, the education system didn't do anything. I actually ran into that principal two weeks ago when I was at a conference in Toronto. There were fifteen hundred people at this luncheon, and I ended up sitting at the table next to her. In front of probably eighteen people who were listening, I told her, "You need to be aware of what you did by ignoring the abuse that happened. You need to know the pain that I went through because you chose to ignore it." She started to cry, and I felt bad for her. But that happened, after all, in the eighties. That was yesterday.

Chapter Eight
Beyond Coming Out Summary of Themes

The Experience of Gay Men

Beyond the initial steps taken to self-identify as gay, as described in chapter six, another phase of development was underway. Without necessarily realizing that it was occurring, we continued our growth as gay individuals. We began establishing a positive gay identity. To reiterate, we were not all headed toward the same destination. We are unique, and part of our growth has been recognizing the complexities of gay identity, and learning to accept the differences that exist in our community. Overall, however, it seems that to become a positive gay individual, three processes leading to the development of a gay identity need to become integrated: connecting with self, connecting with the gay world, and reconnecting with the straight world.

The first process included further changes occurring within our minds. We had to overcome the internal and external oppression which the demon of homophobia launched against us. We viewed our experience as essential to becoming free and liberated. Most of us saw our transformation as giving us the opportunity to become authentic human beings. The threads of our personality became woven into a solid braid as we became whole and complete for the first time. The demon's final demise occurred when fear, hatred, and guilt were replaced with self-love. Self-acceptance became its hallmark, with feeling positive about being gay as its corollary.

With enough of the internal work accomplished, a strength of character developed that allowed us to stand up for our beliefs. Our uniqueness would no longer be suppressed. We could now challenge individuals and society itself with their own demon, one with which we were all too familiar.

The second process leading to integration was our connection with the gay world. We all sought involvement in the gay community by attending gay events, frequenting gay venues, and/or by spending time with gay people. Some of us began this aspect of our journey by strongly identifying with the gay community and allowing it to define who we were as gay men. Some experienced this as becoming saturated by the gay scene. The gay bar, the gay clubs and organizations, the gay-frequented or owned restaurants, and gay friendships became consuming. For most, this level of involvement in the gay subculture diminished over time.

Most of us developed a sense of pride in being gay, with a concurrent desire to celebrate our gay identities. This is exemplified internally by preferring to be gay as compared to straight, and externally by attending gay events like pride marches.

Another way that we connect to the gay world is through intimate relationships. Most of us either desire or are in a partnership with another gay male. Nearly all of us have had the experience of falling in love with a male in the past, and many are currently in love with someone.

Beyond fulfilling our own needs, we have also developed an altruistic spirit, often expressed as a desire to "give something back" to the gay community. Our own healing has taken years, and through this we have developed an empathy for others who are still in need. Aptly described by one individual, we want to act as "Ambassadors of Change" for the gay community. Through its many forms—doing volunteer work, befriending those who need our help, or offering money to gay causes, for example—we aim to make a difference. We try to give voice to those whose voice has been shattered or silenced.

Despite how well we put ourselves together and made inroads in the gay community, we were not living on a gay island removed from civilization. The third process requiring integration was our reconnection with the straight world. We, like you, had already been exposed to the straight world, and perhaps overexposed. We already knew so much about the straight world that during our coming out, many of us had to temporarily abandon it to break its pervasive hold on us. Our return to mainstream society is never the same as we experienced during our initial indoctrination. We have changed.

We are constantly challenged in deciding to whom we wish to disclose. One person described this as our second "coming out," and we never complete this process as there are always new people entering our lives. Most of us have felt that disclosing to others has been helpful in our development of a positive gay identity. However, it would be inaccurate to report that this has occurred without negative consequences. Tragically, many gay men have experienced discrimination, harassment, or even violence because of being identified as visibly gay. Nonetheless, most of us are unwilling to hide anymore, despite the suffering we may need to endure. What we find hard to understand is why we need to suffer at all. We're beautiful people too.

Disclosing to family and trying to work through the shock and trauma that often occurs has also been an important part of building a positive gay identity. Family relationships are often strained for a time. Some parents continue to hold homophobic attitudes while struggling to accept their gay sons. Thankfully, most are eventually able to break the demon's hold on them as well. Unconditional love knows no demons.

We all need to find ways to manage the stigma of being gay. Its consequences can be life threatening. It takes much courage to be gay. This, perhaps more than any other trait, underlies the development of a positive gay identity.

The construction and integration of a positive gay identity is complex and multifaceted. It requires that the self, the gay world, and the straight world become consolidated into our personal identity. The fusion of these three components creates a unique template for each of us. Embedded somewhere is our belief in the basic equality and worth of each person, and each person's journey. We are individuals, and we want to stay that way. Most of us have fought stereotypes all our lives. We were, and still are, sick of them.

Discussion Regarding These Experiences

Connecting with Self

An important theme in developing a positive gay identity is **embracing wholeness.**[47] This results in an integration of the fragmented pieces of identity. Until gay men become whole and complete, their passion, enthusiasm, zest for life, sexual attractions, and love interests are disconnected.[48] This produces feelings of unhappiness, reflecting disengagement from the deepest source of life energy, which is commonly called *libido*.

When identity is fragmented, the ability to empathize with others is hampered. So is the ability to love someone else in a deep, honest, consummate way. The gay man who becomes whole has something to celebrate, something that deserves much recognition. He finally has *himself*.

Another theme is **attaining authenticity.** Peter, for example, went through hell to become an authentic human being. Since his tumultuous coming out, he has become unwilling to be someone else's "dirty little secret," and he is unwilling to take responsibility for other people having trouble accepting him. As he said, "When I saw that people had a hard time dealing with that [his homosexuality], I began to realize that it was their problem, not my problem." Peter won't settle for anything less than complete honesty from himself and from the significant others in his life. He has come a long way from when he used to lie to himself constantly about his sexuality.

A theme regarding positive gay identity that Gavin's story highlights is what I call **becoming free, feeling free.** Everyone I interviewed said this was an important aspect of their experience. Gay men view their coming out as providing them newfound freedom, both to be themselves and to act in ways that they define as appropriate. But this movement toward liberation is often paradoxical in the early stages.

On the one hand, repressed, pent-up feelings are released as coming out allows both emotional and physical expressions of affection to occur with other men. On the other hand, there is still angst in doing this. Feelings of freedom mix with feelings of embarrassment, guilt, and self-doubt. Many at this stage abuse alcohol and drugs to feel free and act free. The old tapes continue playing anything but relaxing music.

Positive gay men have learned to play their own music, however, and its sound is soothing to the soul. **Becoming free, feeling free** is about transcending societal and cultural norms about people, relationships, priorities, values, institutions, and passage rites. It is the freedom to create one's own beliefs and to live according to one's own convictions. In Gavin's words, "Being gay is about freedom from everything—absolute freedom."

A critical theme in the development of a positive gay identity is embracing self-love, which includes three sub-themes: (1)

developing a positive gay schema, (2) feeling positive, and (3) self-acceptance. Self-acceptance occurs when you approve of who you are. Self-love takes this approval to a higher level. With love, you have learned to like yourself and care deeply about what happens to you. It includes deep respect for and commitment to your feelings, thoughts, and actions.

It is hard to imagine the emotional pain that some people experience before they face what their hearts and desires have told them for years. Like the title of Rob Eichberg's book[49] suggests, coming out *is* an act of love. Most psychologists and spiritual leaders accept that loving oneself is a prerequisite to truly loving other people. Until gay men develop a positive identity, their self-esteem and self-concept are continually compromised, and this impairment thwarts their ability to love. Many relationships have faltered because of one or both people's inability to embrace self-love.

David revealed his developing self-acceptance when he stated, "I decided it might be okay to allow myself to be who I am and stop pretending to be someone I wasn't. I kept vacillating, though, until I eventually decided that I have to accept this. It's there and it's just going to make me feel worse if I keep denying it...I had to accept who I was, like it or not." Research indicates that self-acceptance is the single largest predictor of mental health in lesbigay youths.[50] Its importance cannot be over-stated.

David was only sixteen when I interviewed him, yet already he had made tremendous progress in developing self-love. In the interview he said, "Now the thought of being straight seems so boring to me." He is also beginning to drop innuendos at school so others might suspect he is gay. By testing his surroundings, David is getting a better sense if others will approve of him. At his age, approval from others is an important aspect of learning to love himself.

Self-love does not require continuing love from other people to flourish, however.[51] Everybody will not lavish the gay man with praise when he eventually discloses to them. Some, in fact, may reject him outright, either temporarily or permanently. Positive gay men have learned to courageously face other people's reactions to their coming-out disclosure. That takes a lot of self-love.

The two remaining sub-themes of self-love are **developing a positive gay schema** and **feeling positive.** "I identify being a positive gay person with being a positive person in general..." Matthew stated. "Any issue can be approached with either a positive mindset or a negative mindset." Developing a positive gay identity is much easier for individuals who can see the positive side of a situation or life circumstance. As a popular metaphor demonstrates, whether we see a cup as half-empty or half-full is a matter of perception. Both are accurate perceptions, but one leaves us feeling lacking, while the other leaves us feeling hopeful.

In reality, there is no such thing as absolute truth. The many beliefs and lifestyles of people throughout the world testify to this relativity. Positive gay men adopt a philosophy of truth that is healthy. Whenever possible, they see the cup as half full.

For example, acquiring the HIV virus did not diminish Fréderic's sense of having a positive gay identity—it strengthened it. People grow when they are challenged, when they have to develop coping skills to deal with adversity. After finding out he was HIV positive, Fréderic said, "My world didn't collapse. Instead, I entered a new coming out process." He later stated, "I am now two kinds of gay positive. I am the positive gay and HIV positive."

Fréderic was able to give his HIV status personal meaning, thereby elevating his struggle to a spiritual level. Gay men with positive identities see a purpose in their fight. Belief in oneself, and in a higher power or purpose, is beneficial to mental health.

Another important theme is **embracing and releasing personal power**, which includes the following three sub-themes: **(1) timing and readiness, (2) developing strength of character and autonomous thinking,** and **(3) standing up for one's beliefs.** John provided a good example of empowerment. When the time was right, he became an outspoken and powerful advocate of gay liberation. As revealed in his story, John's profession and charisma led him "into some very positive appointments to various committees and boards and so forth where it was known that [he] was a gay person."

Unlike John, most gay men don't influence others at the federal political level. Nonetheless, positive gay men find ways to embrace and release their personal power. For example, Matthew had a profound effect on his Mennonite family, Peter helped alter the views of local politicians, and Fréderic helped shape some gay people's views about HIV. Each positive gay man has created a significant impact within his circle of influence.

The **timing and readiness** of when one chooses to embrace and release their personal power is an important consideration. Andrew, for example, succinctly stated his perspective: "Readiness is an important point here. My disclosure to others and my immersion did not occur until I was in a place of power, where the cost wouldn't outweigh the benefit. When I started learning about my history as a gay man, it had a lot to do with my development and my identification with gay politics."

Positive gay men have come to listen carefully to the clues that inform them that the time is right for disclosure or action. To disclose one's gayness to a group of drunken bikers is foolhardy. Letting a government write antigay legislation without rebuttal is as well. There is a time and place to speak up, act up, and shut up. That stance remains prudent until the oppression of gay people has fully ended.

I've mentioned before that it takes great courage to be openly gay. The sub-theme that speaks to this courage is called **developing strength of character and autonomous thinking**. Fréderic exemplified this theme in the *Before Coming Out* section of this book, where he stated, "I need to define my own gayness because I am somebody who believes strongly in my own independence and in my own self-determination." Like a true artist, Fréderic painted his own story and lived it. Up close, one could see many flaws in the canvas. From a distance, one witnessed a masterpiece in progress.

Strength of character, autonomous thinking, and courage provide the fuel for the work that needs to be done to build a positive gay identity. The remaining sub-theme related to these is *standing up for one's beliefs*. Tommy, for example, became assertive about his gay identity when he and two others formed the first gay organization at his university. He later pounced and fought with a guy who was ripping down their posters. Later he published his own gay newspaper.

Before Tommy could take action, he had to be comfortable with his development as a positive gay person. Just as there are many different personality types, there are also many different types of actions one can take. For example, introverts may prefer to disclose to only a few of their closest friends and family members, whereas extroverts may feel comfortable sharing with many more individuals. Whatever one's personality, **standing up for one's beliefs** is easier for those who know they have every right to be who *they* are.

Connecting with the Gay World

Besides the inner work that needs to be done, the positive gay man also finds ways to connect with the gay world. Two themes that Alex's story exemplifies are **gaining a collective sense of identity** and **celebrating gayness (i.e., gay pride)**. The importance of gay pride was considered so significant by a noted gay theorist[52] that it represented the fifth stage of identity development in her theory. Gay men exemplify gay pride and celebration by attending gay events, gay marches, and other behaviors that indicate joy in being gay. Alex expressed it as follows: "I'm very proud of being gay. I'm planning to get a rainbow band tattooed on my arm with the word pride underneath...I live a relatively gay lifestyle, I support gay organizations, I shop in gay businesses, I support my community..."

Since 1969, the view of homosexuality has shifted from that of "an individual condition to a collective identity."[53] Researchers have argued that all individuals in marginalized groups need to develop both a collective identity and an individual identity.[54] **Gaining a collective sense of identity** refers to men feeling that the gay community defines part of their personal identity.

"By this point, I was a flamer," said Alex. "I was hanging out with incredibly queer people, and I was beginning to get a sense of queer identity." Building a collective or group identity is problematic, however, as it is never clear who has the authority to define the components or parameters of it.[55]

One could emphasize the many factions within the gay community, for example, in an attempt to define the collective, including groups like the drag queens, the leathermen, and the bears. Kevin Dilallo and Jack Krumholtz in their humorous satire, *The Unofficial Gay Manual*,[56] refer to thirteen "stereotypes" in the gay world: the biker, the pib (i.e., person in black), the club kid, the opera queen, the activist, the poodle, the a-lister, the bohemian, the boy next door, the cowboy, the clone, the sugar daddy, and the gym dandy. Neither deserves description here, but the humor in such a classification scheme reminds us not only of the stereotypes that still exist, both within and outside the gay community, but also of the individual differences.

There is not one collective identity with a singular set of beliefs and norms. Rather, many collective identities can help define gay people. The main point of such affiliation is that gay people feel connected to others who are also gay.

A recurring theme in the experience of gay men who develop positive identities is their continued **involvement in the gay community**. Research clearly indicates that involvement in the gay community is helpful to gay people's psychological health and functioning.[57] Social support eases the tension of living in a homophobic world.

Involvement may take many forms. The gay bar remains the most popular venue for socializing,[58] but additional choices include frequenting other gay establishments (e.g., restaurants, retail stores, coffee houses), attending gay events, house parties, clubs and organizations, and hanging out with gay friends. Living in a community with large percentages of gay people is yet another option.

The extent of this involvement varies greatly between individuals and for any particular individual. The same person may saturate himself with involvement in the gay community at one point, and then later "disappear" for a while. Andrew described a period of saturation when he stated, "The immersion thing happened for me while I worked in the gay bar. While I was there, I think I lost a really important chunk of the rest of my community—like straight friends and school friends. There was a period of about a year-and-a-half where I don't think I did much socially with people who weren't gay."

In the gay world, no established norm or rule dictates how much involvement is considered appropriate or necessary. How much one chooses to become involved is an individual choice. There is no script that need be followed.

Another way that people connect to the gay world is through **pursuing or having relationships**. Paul was on a suicide mission, driving his car off the highway to meet a horrible end when he paused momentarily. In that moment, he realized that he deserved to live. As his own inner healing proceeded, he soon met the one man who would take his heart for the rest of his life.

Not every gay man desires a deep, intimate relationship, but the majority do. Most would like to feel the incredible love that Paul felt for his partner.

Nearly all of the positive gay men I interviewed wanted to give something back to the gay community. Most already had made a contribution in one area or another. I borrowed the label for this theme from Frank, who called this **acting as an ambassador of change**. Frank, for example, was an active volunteer in gay causes. When gay people come to deeply love themselves, they often want to share their knowledge and good feeling with others. This positive energy leads them to help in whatever way they can. These continuing contributions have made a tremendous difference in helping to replace the myths of homosexuality with the truth, for both gay people and heterosexuals alike.

Reconnecting with the Straight World

Most gay men do not live on islands, away from heterosexual society. Consequently, part of developing a positive gay identity will entail finding ways to reconnect with the straight world.

Disclosing to others is an important theme in developing a positive gay identity. Much research and writing has been dedicated to the effects of disclosure on gay identity and psychological health. Generally, the research suggests that disclosure contributes to better psychological adjustment and enhancement of a positive gay identity.[59]

There are certain cautions, however. Before gay men disclose to everyone they know, they need to consider the potential impact. The impact—both their own and on the people they tell—will depend on several factors, including race, ethnicity, class, age, geographic location, religion, occupation, and community support.[60] Disclosing one's gayness to someone may engender several possible reactions, ranging from complete acceptance to absolute rejection and potential violence. Many lesbigay youths have been verbally, physically, and sexually abused by family members and peers.[61] There is no substitute for careful discernment.

"I have not had a bad experience with anyone that I have come out to," explained
Troy. "It has all been very positive." An earlier girlfriend accepted his gayness and they remained friends. Although Troy's mother became his greatest supporter, his father continued struggling with accepting him as gay.

Disclosing to others is an ongoing process. Beyond deciding whether to tell those closest to them, there are always new faces coming into the lives of gay people. Each time a gay man lies to someone, however, he does a small disservice to himself. The inner message to oneself is something like, "I shouldn't be myself because this person might not accept me" or "I shouldn't love myself." Generally, positive gay men only lie about their gayness when it would prove highly disadvantageous to do otherwise.

The ultimate step in disclosing is going public, which involves disclosing to a public audience. This is a step that relatively few gay men take in life.[62] Jerome's decision to stand out and speak after the bathhouse raid broke a silence that has been pervasive throughout society.

Breaking the silence may bring consequences, however, and this theme I call **managing the consequences of external homophobia (e.g., harassment, violence).** Positive gay men must discover ways to do this, and we must protect ourselves as well. Forty percent of the men I interviewed acknowledged that they had suffered some form of discrimination, harassment, or violence because of being gay. Jerome admitted that he had been physically assaulted twice because he is gay. He had suffered intense harassment as well.

The external consequences are often more subtle. Some examples include witnessing how a person recoils slightly when you mention you are gay; not getting a job promotion when you are the most qualified person; and being either ignored by people or excluded from their conversation. *Heterosexism* is yet another consequence of external homophobia, which are the many ways individuals in our society consciously or unconsciously minimize gay people, either by assuming that they don't exist or by projecting a belief that they are somehow inferior compared with their heterosexual counterparts.

Here are a few examples of heterosexism: (1) when teachers talk about relationships, and only mention opposite-sex coupling arrangements; (2) when parents ask their son if he has a girlfriend yet, instead of asking if he is dating [someone] yet; and (3) when a gay couple checks into a hotel and the clerk automatically assigns a room with two beds. Sometimes heterosexism is subtle, like in the first example, and sometimes it is just plain rude, like in the third example.

A related theme to disclosing is **dealing with family and significant others.** Dealing with family is a special challenge for most gay men. Most parents initially react negatively when their son comes out to them. Such reactions can range from mild annoyance and disappointment to verbal abuse and violence. Luckily, the initial shock generally subsides and is replaced with some degree of acceptance. Over time, many relationships between parents and gay sons are enhanced through the disclosure.[63] Their relationship often improves as a direct result of the greater honesty. Despite this generalization, several co-researchers continued to struggle with some degree of family strife and conflict.

Positive gay men are prepared to face the consequences of their authenticity, even if that means having to sever ties with some people once thought to be "close." How close is someone who cannot love the very thing that makes a person so unique, loving, and passionate? It is not easy to love oneself in the midst of such oppression, but nonetheless, there is no room for compromise.

The Consolidation of Identity

Eventually in the development of a positive gay identity, an integration of perspectives occurs. I call this the **consolidation of identity**. Before this happens, the gay male has made significant achievements in three areas: **(1) connecting with self; (2) connecting with the gay world; and (3) reconnecting with the straight world.** Each of these include themes that have already been discussed. Becoming a positive gay man is about one's unique way of constructing a viable, healthy identity.

Glenn's comments articulate this consolidation of identity. "That's where I'm at now in terms of positive gay identity; being gay is merely one petal on the flower, and that is a part of the whole. It's no more or no less important than any other aspect of who I am...Above all, I am a human being with human issues. I also happen to be gay."

Don't get the wrong impression. Glenn is not a perfectly self-actualized gay man. Nobody is. We are all struggling to make sense of our experience and continually working at becoming better people. Isn't that true for all of us, gay or straight?

Alex, for example, succumbed to a life of prostitution, alcohol, and drugs during his adolescence. His story serves to clarify an important distinction: having a positive gay identity is not the same thing as having optimal mental health. Being gay is not a mental disorder, but gay people can suffer from mental disorders like anyone else. Depression, for example, afflicts people worldwide, despite race, ethnic origin, color, gender, or sexual orientation.

Although positive gay identity and optimal mental health are discrete constructs, they are related. For example, the establishment of a positive gay identity is important in fostering better mental health for gay men and lesbian women.[64] Positive gay men have more positive self-concepts, better self-esteem, and are generally lower in anxiety and depression compared to men with negative gay identities.[65]

In summary, having a positive gay identity generally enhances one's mental health, but it does not guarantee freedom from mental health problems that have nothing to do with one's gayness. Similarly, having optimal mental health does not suggest that the individual has done the necessary work required to develop a positive gay identity either.

Chapter Nine
Beyond and Back

"If I am nothing but what I believe I am supposed to be—who am I'?"
(Fromm, 1969/1941, p. 280).

Personal Reflections

I shared with you in chapter two the definitions of positive gay identity provided by the co-researchers. Now let me share with you what I have learned, which is incorporated into my definition of what it means to have developed a positive gay identity:

Individuals who have attained a positive gay identity have developed a high self-regard for themselves as gay persons. They view their gay status as equal to straight status. If given a choice, they would not prefer to be straight over gay, for they have come to value their uniqueness, and the richness of life that comes from being themselves. They have integrated their gay identity with their other identities, and having accomplished this, they are "out" in most areas of their lives, wherever and whenever it is not highly disadvantageous to do so. They have largely overcome their own internalized homophobia, which frees them to fully love others of the same gender.

I also learned that I can only enter a room when I am ready to accept what is inside it. Before then, the door is locked. Even a frantic attempt to open it meets only with frustration and despair.

I opened the door to my own coming out seven years ago. Since then, I have had the privilege of talking to others about how they faced what was inside their closet. I feel deeply blessed that I was allowed to hear their stories, feel their pain, and experience their joy. Each co-researcher reminded me of the communality of our lived experiences.

Working through my research has at times been more fulfilling and upsetting than I would have expected. Some gay men talk about disclosing to others as their "second coming out." Doing this work has felt like a third. I again rode the roller-coaster as I learned about theory, engaged in counseling practice, interviewed co-researchers, wrote about their experiences, and simultaneously lived my own. I was unprepared for the intensity.

One of my co-researchers correctly intuited one of my motivations for researching this topic. I too needed to learn more about developing a positive gay identity. No one has it all together. I can only hope now that what I have learned will be of benefit to many of us. This work, after all, has been part of my salvation, and part of my giving back to the gay community.

Update on the Co-researchers

I kept in contact with some of the co-researchers after the interviews. This is what I know about them currently:

Matthew, 32

Matthew now lives in Vancouver, and he has found what he so earnestly sought—a life partner. He is happy and, as always, positive in his outlook on life.

Peter, 40

Peter persists in his battle against the stereotypes and misconceptions about gay men in both his personal and professional life. He continues to support gay causes.

Frank, 38

I periodically see Frank in the community, but we haven't talked for a long time. I heard from one source that Frank will soon be moving to Eastern Canada. Calgary will miss him.

Gavin, 32

Gavin continues to work for himself in business. He also has been involved in a satisfying relationship with a younger man.

Jonathan, 30

Jonathan still works as a systems analyst, frequently traveling as part of his job. He is deeply committed to a man he met shortly before our interview.

Jerome, 48

Jerome remains an out politician re-elected twice in a major city. We have also stayed in touch with each other since the interview.

Fréderic, 38

Three months after our interview, I walked into a huge room brimming over with hundreds of men, women, and children, unsure if I was in the right place. Why are there so many children? Children's drawings were everywhere, and off center were large replicas of crayons that symbolized his art. The music played Pachelbel while I took one of the few seats left at the back. Fréderic had passed away suddenly, peacefully, and unexpectedly.

I discovered that he was a man who had touched many lives. He loved life, and he made people laugh with a sense of humor that was nearly insane. I can see why so many people loved him.

The ninety minute bilingual memorial was a celebration. I don't understand French and didn't need to, to understand the impact of this man. The words were only the surface for a depth that I and hundreds of others admired. There were more laughs than I had expected. Seated in the back row was one who wasn't yet ready to laugh. He hadn't yet had enough time to grieve this remarkable man whom he knew for only three hours. Thank you, God, for three hours.

Tommy, 41

I lost contact with Tommy soon after finishing my dissertation. I believe he resides in Calgary, but I haven't seen him for nearly two years.

Cliff, 30

Occasionally I run into Cliff, and he is now only minimally involved in doing drag shows. He remains well-known, however, by those in the gay community.

Paul, 50

Six months after interviewing Paul, I had coffee with the psychologist who referred him to me. My body chilled as she told me that he had died suddenly and unexpectedly four days earlier. At his request, there would not be a memorial. I was used to death, but Paul had become *my* role model, and I grieved him more than I thought I should, having only known him for four hours. As I'm sure Roger, his partner, would attest, however—he was easy to love.

John, 61

Our connection was deep, and it did not surprise me that we became close friends after I graduated. Only days after having him over for dinner a few months later, he died from cancer. I still don't have words to describe my sense of loss, and even now I sometimes find myself overwhelmed with grief. He had become the gay father I needed then.

David, 16

David had asked me where could he meet other young gay teenagers like himself. He already knew about the gay youth group, and had attended it, but he wanted to meet still more gay youth. Even then, I admired his tenacity, so I was not surprised to hear a few months later that he and his mother started their own gay youth group. Hats off to you, David!

Glenn, 46

Glenn's involvement with the leather community fascinated me. His friendship still does. He works in the same job as before, but hopes to make some radical life changes over the next few years.

Troy, 24

The last contact I had with Troy was shortly before his return to Ontario. I haven't heard anything about him since.

Andrew, 29

Although I lost contact with Andrew shortly after our interview, I heard from someone else that he continues working for a nonprofit organization.

Alex, 23

Alex returned to a life of drugs and alcohol at some point

following our interview. A number of months later, he again took steps toward recovery, and found the strength to become "clean." Nonetheless, he continued struggling to make sense of his troublesome past. Yesterday is not easily forgotten. Nor has it been for any of us.

We have a great deal to look forward to as positive gay men, however. We are gay, and we have every reason to celebrate it. I hope, by now, you understand why.

Final Thoughts

Quoting Shannon and Woods, "the importance of establishing a positive gay identity cannot be overstated (191, p. 198)." The cost of not developing a positive identity is staggering to gay people, and to society at large. Many personal difficulties have been associated with remaining in denial of one's sexual orientation, and in failing to develop a positive gay identity after coming out. Those afflicted have paid an incredible price to try to be something they are not. It takes incredible courage to recognize one's difference, to act upon it, and then to celebrate it. This book has been about the courage and determination of men who have become free enough of societal oppression that they can see, hear, feel, touch, and taste another way of living.

The gay-affirmative view is that we are equal: being gay is no better and no worse than being straight. It sounds like an easy place to get to, yet nothing could be further from the truth. Although significant progress regarding human rights legislation for gay men and lesbians is occurring in Canada, gay people continue to suffer discrimination and harassment from others. Disparaging remarks are still heard. The pervasive code of silence still mutes our voices. Even caged animals will eventually retaliate. We have been caged long enough.

Positive gay identity is about liberation, inspiration, courage, strength, nonconformity, acceptance of self, acceptance of others, uniqueness, and love. That which grows from within flowers and becomes visible to everyone who takes notice. The *"love that dare not speak its name,"* as Oscar Wilde called it, now *has* a name. The positive gay man loves others insomuch as he loves himself. It's about time we help him to do so.

Coming out can initially feel like the singular most lonely act a gay man has ever experienced. If you are one of them, relax. *Beyond* coming out lies a whole world of opportunity, people, unique identities, and pride in successfully achieving an integrated identity. Remember that "a journey of a thousand miles must begin with a single step."[66] The first step is often the hardest.

Endnotes

1. Hershberger & D'Augelli (1995).

2. Savin-Williams (1994).

3. Rotheram-Borus & Fernandez (1995).

4. Malyon (1982b); and McFarland (1993).

5. Malyon (1982a).

6. Kus (1988).

7. Martin (1982); Nardi (1995); and Taylor (1985).

8. *Coming out* is a term that has multiple meanings in the literature and in the vernacular. In this book, it refers to the process of self-identifying as gay.

9. *Co-researcher* is another term for *interviewee*. The term better acknowledges the significant role that each interviewee has in this type of research.

10. *Coding* is a technique used to help extract common themes from the interview transcripts. *Internalized homophobia* is an example of a common theme with gay people.

11. *Nellie* is a colloquial term meaning "effeminate."

12. Friedman & Downey (1994); Isay (1996); and Troiden (1979).

13. Money (1988); and Rosario, Meyer-Bahlburg, Hunter, Exner, Gwadz, & Keller (1996).

14. Isay (1996, p. 79).

15. Isay (1988, p. 44).

16. Sternberg (1986).

17. Cass (1983-84).

18. Vargo (1998).

19. Bagley & Tremblay (1998).

20. Blumenfeld & Raymond (1993).

21. See Isay (1996); and Nicolosi (1991).

22. Beard & Glickauf-Hughes (1994); and Gonsiorek, Sell, & Weinrich (1995).

23. Haldeman (1994); and Murphy (1992).

24. Kottman, Lingg, & Tisdell (1995); Olson & King (1995); and Rotheram-Borus & Fernandez (1995).

25. Dubay (1987, p. 102).

26. Hart (1981).

27. Beard & Glickauf-Hughes (1994).

28. Lee (1977).

29. Hetrick & Martin (1984).

30. Hetrick & Martin (1987).

31. Kottman, Lingg, & Tisdell (1995); and Telljohann, Price, Poureslami, & Easton (1995).

32. Malyon (1982b).

33. Helminiak (1994); Herdt (1997); and Herrman (1990).

34. Herdt (1997).

35. Herdt (1997, p. 70).

36. Bailey, Bobrow, Wolfe, & Mikach (1995); Bozett (1993); Garnets & Kimmel (1993); and Patterson (1995).

37. Bailey, Bobrow, Wolfe, & Mikach (1995); Bigner & Bozett (1989); and Gottman (1989).

38. Dank (1971).

39. Barrows & Halgin (1988); Beane (1981); and Fassinger (1991).

40. Kroger (1996).

41. Money (1988).

42. Isay (1996).

43. Hammersmith & Weinberg (1973).

44. A new word used to describe individuals who are either lesbian, gay, or bisexual.

45. The T4 count is one measure of the body's ability to fight infection.

46 S/M, S&M or sado-masochism

47. Cornett (1995).

48. Isay (1996).

49. Eichberg (1990).

50. Hershberger & D'Augelli (1995).

51. Ellis & Harper (1975).

52. Cass (1979).

53. Garnets & Kimmel (1993, p. 599).

54. Cox & Gallois (1996).

55. Gamson (1995).

56. Dilallo & Krumholtz (1994).

57. D'Augelli (1991); Leserman, DiSantostefano, Perkins, & Evans (1994); Minton & McDonald (1983-84); and Walters & Simoni (1993).

58. Shannon & Woods (1991).

59. Garnets, Herek, & Levy (1990); Lesserman, DiSantostefano, Perkins, & Evans (1994); and Schmitt & Kurdek (1987).

60. Fassinger & Miller (1996).

61. Savin-Williams (1994).

62. Lee (1977).

63. Cramer & Roach (1988).

64. Leserman, DiSantostefano, Perkins, & Evans (1994); and Miranda & Storms (1989).

65. Schmitt & Kurdek (1987).

66. Lao Tzu, father of Taoism, 604 - 531 BC.

References

Bagley, C., & Tremblay, P. (1998). On the prevalence of homosexuality and bisexuality, in a random community survey of 750 men aged 18 to 27. *Journal of Homosexuality, 36*, (2), 1-18.

Bailey, J. M., Bobrow, D., Wolfe, M., & Mikach, S. (1995). Sexual orientation of adult sons of gay fathers. *Developmental Psychology, 31*, 124-129.

Barrows, P. A., & Halgin, R. P. (1988). Current issues in psychotherapy with gay men: Impact of the AIDS phenomenon. *Professional Psychology: Research and Practice, 19*, 395-402.

Bass, E., & Davis. L. (1992). *The courage to heal: A guide for women survivors of child sexual abuse.* New York, NY: Harper Collins, p. 168.

Beane, J. (1981). "I'd rather be dead than gay": Counseling gay men who are coming out. *The Personnel and Guidance Journal, 60,* 222-226.

Beard, J., & Glickauf-Hughes, C. (1994). Gay identity and sense of self: Rethinking male homosexuality. *Journal of Gay & Lesbian Psychotherapy, 2* (2), 21-37.

Bigner, J. J., & Bozett, F. W. (1989). Parenting by gay fathers. *Marriage and Family Review, 14* (3-4), 155-175.

Blumenfeld, W. J., & Raymond, D. (1993). *Looking at gay and lesbian life* (updated and expanded edition). Boston, MA: Beacon Press.

Bozett, F. W. (1993). Gay fathers: A review of the literature. In L. D. Garnets & D. C. Kimmel (Eds.), *Psychological perspectives on lesbian and gay male experiences* (pp. 437-457). New York, NY: Columbia University Press.

Cass, V. C. (1979). Homosexual identity formation: A theoretical model. *Journal of Homosexuality, 4,* 219-235.

Cass, V. C. (1983-84). Homosexual identity: A concept in need of definition. *Journal of Homosexuality, 9,* 105-126.

Cornett, C. (1995). *Reclaiming the authentic self: Dynamic psychotherapy with gay men.* Northvale, NJ: Jason Aronson.

Cox, S., & Gallois, C. (1996). Gay and lesbian identity development: A social identity perspective. *Journal of Homosexuality, 30* (4), 1-30.

Cramer, D. W., & Roach, A. S. (1988). Coming out to mom and dad: A study of gay males and their relationships with their parents. *Journal of Homosexuality, 15* (3-4), 79-91.

Dank, B. M. (1971). Coming out in the gay world. *Psychiatry, 34,* 180-197.

D'Augelli, A. R. (1991). Gay men in college: Identity processes and adaptations. *Journal of College Student Development, 32,* 140-146.

Dilallo, K., & Krumholtz (1994). *The Unofficial Gay Manual.* New York, NY: Doubleday.

DuBay, W. H. (1987). *Gay identity: The self under ban.* Jefferson, NC: McFarland & Co.

Eichberg, R. (1990). *Coming out: An act of love.* New York, NY: Plume.

Ellis, A., & Harper, R. A. (1975). *A new guide to rational living.* Englewood Cliffs, NJ: Prentice-Hall, Inc.

Fassinger, R. E. (1991). The hidden minority: Issues and challenges in working with lesbian women and gay men. *The Counseling Psychologist, 19,* 157-176.

Fassinger, R. E., & Miller, B. A. (1996). Validation of an inclusive model of sexual minority identity formation on a sample of gay men. *Journal of Homosexuality, 32* (2), 53-78.

Friedman, R. C., & Downey, J. I. (1994). Special article: Homosexuality. *New England Journal of Medicine, 331* (4), 923-930.

Fromm, E. (1969/1941). *Escape from freedom.* New York, NY: Holt, Reinhart and Winston.

Gamson, J. (1995). Must identity movements self-destruct? A queer dilemma. *Social Problems, 42,* 390-407.

Garnets, L., Herek, G.M., & Levy, B. (1990). Violence and victimization of lesbians and gay men: Mental health consequences. *Journal of Interpersonal Violence, 5,* 366-383.

Garnets, L. D., & Kimmel, D. C. (1993). Introduction: Lesbian and gay male dimensions in the psychological study of human diversity. In L. D. Garnets & D. C. Kimmel (Eds.), *Psychological perspectives on lesbian and gay male experiences* (pp. 1-51). New York, NY: Columbia University Press.

Gonsiorek, J. C., Sell, R. L., & Weinrich, J. D. (1995). Definition and measurement of sexual orientation. *Suicide and Life-Threatening Behavior, 25, supplement 95,* 40-51.

Gottman, J. S. (1989). Children of gay and lesbian parents. *Marriage and Family Review, 14* (3-4), 177-196.

Haldeman, D. C. (1994). The practice and ethics of sexual orientation conversion therapy. *Journal of Consulting and Clinical Psychology, 62,* 221-227.

Hammersmith, S. K., & Weinberg, M. S. (1973). Homosexual identity: Commitment, adjustments, and significant others. *Sociometry, 36,* (1), 56-78.

Hart, J. (1981). Self and professional help. In J. Hart & D. Richardson (Eds.), *The theory and practice of homosexuality.* (pp. 128-138). Boston, MA: Routledge & Kegan Paul.

Helminiak, D. A. (1994). *What the Bible really says about homosexuality*. San Francisco, CA: Alamo Square Press.

Herdt, G. (1997). *Same sex, different cultures*. Boulder, CO: Westview Press.

Herrman, B. (1990). *Being - being happy - being gay*. San Francisco, CA: Alamo Square Press.

Hershberger, S. L., & D'Augelli, A. R. (1995). The impact of victimization on the mental health and suicidality of lesbian, gay, and bisexual youths. *Developmental Psychology, 31*, 65-74.

Hetrick, E. S., & Martin, A. D. (1984). Ego-dystonic homosexuality: A developmental view. In E. S. Herrick & T. S. Stein (Eds.), *Innovations in psychotherapy with homosexuals.* (pp. 1-21). Washington, DC: American Psychiatric Press.

Hetrick, E. S., & Martin, A. D. (1987). Developmental issues and their resolution for gay and lesbian adolescents. *Journal of Homosexuality, 14* (1/2), 25-43.

Isay, R. A. (1988). Homosexuality in heterosexual and homosexual men. *Psychiatric Annals, 18*, 43-46.

Isay, R. A. (1996). *Becoming gay: The journey to self-acceptance*. New York, NY: Pantheon Books.

Kottman, T., Lingg, M., & Tisdell, T. (1995). Gay and lesbian adolescents: Implications for Adlerian Therapists. *Individual Psychology, 51*, 115-128.

Kroger, J. (1996). *Identity in adolescence: The balance between self and other* (2nd ed.). New York, NY: Routledge.

Kurtz, E., & Ketcham, K. (1996). *The spirituality of imperfection: Storytelling and the journey to wholeness*. New York: Bantam Books.

Kus, R. J. (1988). Alcoholism and non-acceptance of gay self: The critical link. *Journal of Homosexuality, 15*, 25-41.

Lee, J. A. (1977). Going public: A study in the sociology of homosexual liberation. *Journal of Homosexuality, 3*, 49-78.

Leserman, J., DiSantostefano, R., Perkins, D. O., & Evans, D. L. (1994). Gay identification and psychological health in HIV-positive and HIV-negative gay men. *Journal of Applied Social Psychology, 24*, 2193-2208.

Malyon, A. K. (1982a). Biphasic aspects of homosexual identity formation. *Psychotherapy: Theory, Research, and Practice, 19*, 335-340.

Malyon, A. K. (1982b). Psychotherapeutic implications of internalized homophobia in gay men. *Journal of Homosexuality, 7* (2-3), 59-69.

Martin, A. D. (1982). Learning to hide: The socialization of the gay adolescent. *Adolescent Psychiatry, 10*, 52-65.

Maupin, A. (date of publication unavailable). Design for living. *Advocate*, p. 41, 93.

McFarland, W. P. (1993). A developmental approach to gay and lesbian youth. *Journal of Humanistic Education and Development, 32*, 17-29.

Minton, H. L., & McDonald, G. J. (1983-84). Homosexual identity formation as a developmental process. *Journal of Homosexuality, 9* (2-3), 91-104.

Miranda, J., & Storms, M. (1989). Psychological adjustment of lesbians and gay men. *Journal of Counseling and Development, 68*, 41-45.

Money, J. (1988). *Gay, straight, and in-between: The sexology of erotic orientation*. New York, NY: Oxford University Press.

Murphy, T. (1992). Redirecting sexual orientation: Techniques and justifications. *Journal of Sex Research, 29,* 501-523.

Nardi, P. M. (1995). AThe breastplate of righteousness": Twenty-five years after Laud Humphreys' *tearoom trade: impersonal sex in public places. Journal of Homosexuality, 30* (2), 1-10.

Nicolosi, J. (1991). *Reparative therapy of male homosexuality: A new clinical approach.* Northvale, NJ: Jason Aronson Inc.

O'Conor, A. (1995). Breaking the silence: Writing about gay, lesbian, and bisexual teenagers. In G. Unks (Ed.), *The gay teen: Educational practice and theory for lesbian, gay and bisexual adolescents.* (pp. 13-15). New York, NY: Routledge.

Olson, E. D., & King, C. A. (1995). Gay and lesbian self-identification: A response to Rotheram-Borus and Fernandez. *Suicide and Life-Threatening Behavior, 25,* supplement 95, 35-39.

Otis, M. D., & Skinner, W. F. (1996). The prevalence of victimization and its effects on mental well-being among lesbian and gay people. *Journal of Homosexuality, 30* (3), 93-121.

Page, S., & Yee, M. (1986). Conception of male and female homosexual stereotypes among university undergraduates. *Journal of Homosexuality, 12* (1), 109-118.

Patterson, C. J. (1995). Sexual orientation and human development: An overview. *Developmental Psychology, 31,* 3-11.

Rosario, M, Meyer-Bahlburg, H. F. L., Hunter, J., Exner, T. M., Gwadz, M., & Keller (1996). The psychosexual development of urban lesbian, gay, and bisexual youths. *Journal of Sex Research, 33* (2), 113-126.

Rotheram-Borus, M. J., & Fernandez, M. I. (1995). Sexual orientation and developmental challenges experienced by gay and lesbian youths. *Suicide and Life-Threatening Behavior, 25,* supplement 95, 26-34.

Savin-Williams, R. C. (1994). Verbal and physical abuse as stressors in the lives of lesbian, gay male, and bisexual youths: Associations with school problems, running away, substance abuse, prostitution, and suicide. *Journal of Consulting and Clinical Psychology, 62*, 261-269.

Schmitt, J. P., & Kurdek, L. A. (1987). Personality correlates of positive identity and relationship involvement in gay men. *Journal of Homosexuality, 13* (4), 101-109.

Shannon, J. W., & Woods, W. J. (1991). Affirmative psychotherapy for gay men. *The Counseling Psychologist, 19* (2), 197-215.

Sternberg, R. J. (1986). A triangular theory of love. *Psychological Review, 93*, 119-135.

Taylor, C. L. (1985). Mexican male homosexual interaction in public contexts. *Journal of Homosexuality, 11*, 117-136.

Telljohann, S., Price, J., Poureslami, M., & Easton, A. (1995). Teaching about sexual orientation by secondary health teachers. *Journal of School Health, 65* (1), 18-22.

Troiden, R. R. (1979). Becoming homosexual: A model of gay identity acquisition. *Psychiatry, 42*, 362-373.

Vargo, M. E. (1998). *Acts of disclosure: The coming-out process of contemporary gay men.* Binghamton, NY: Harrington Park Press.

Walters, K. L., & Simoni, J. M. (1993). Lesbian and gay male group identity attitudes and self-esteem: Implications for counseling. *Journal of Counseling Psychology, 40*, 94-99.